KEN'S W

HITLER DEAD... GONE FOR A I

CW00433590

FOREWORD

Kenneth Stanley Haslett was born on 18th October 1928 and lived
all his life within a hundred yards or so of the street he was born
in (Bristol Street, Newport, South Wales). He was aged 10 when the
Second World War broke out and 16 when it ended. His father was
a sergeant-major in the army and was therefore absent from Ken's
life for almost all of the war. During 1942 and 1943, Ken kept a diary.
They describe the life of a working-class teenage boy in the days when
most of a teenager's life happened out of doors and attending Sunday
School was a significant event in the social calendar.

The anecdotes contained in the diaries have been the cause of much
joyful laughter within the family and provided a particularly poignant
memoir following Ken's death in August 2006. Ken's brother, Keith
(whose birth on 14th March 1943 gets a mention in the diary: "Mam
was taken in the night") has transcribed the diaries and provided
footnotes to help those of us who are too young to remember the
"Happidrome" radio series or to know how long a perch is.
We feel that they are worthy of publication and hope you agree.

Christopher Haslett *(Ken's son)*
March, 2010

THE 1940S DIARIES OF A WORKING-CLASS TEENAGER

BY KENNETH HASLETT

MAY 1943

Sunday 2

Got up 9.45. Dox Helped in
in morn. In afternoon gave
bike V.G. cleaning
In evening went out
back & played n.o.s with
S & Marie Bootyoo
Bailey. Tx 8.50. Bed 9.20.

signed KS

P.S. I broke my glasses

TRANSCRIBER'S NOTE

These diaries were hand-written by my brother, Ken, when he was thirteen and fourteen years of age. In transcribing them sixty-seven years later I found myself to be constantly torn between typing exactly what was written and expanding abbreviations, correcting spelling so that people reading it today can understand what was said.

I have always tried to leave it as Ken wrote but sometimes it seemed absolutely necessary to clarify. Examples are "done Fr homework". This is written here as "done Fr[ench] homework" and "7 lbs of Gen Fert" is written as "7 lbs of Gen[eral] Fert[iliser]". It is hoped that the sense of the meaning is not changed.

Reading the diaries, I did get the sense that Ken meant them to be read by someone else in the future. He himself put explanatory notes in brackets and even questioned his own spelling and memory as in "went to see "The Lady Vanishes (Vanished?)"" and "Topliss (prefect) put me in detention". In those cases the brackets are Ken's. Where I have felt compelled to add some further explanation I have started my comments with my initials, KLH.

I hope you get some of the enjoyment and sense of privilege at revisiting a lost time through these diaries.

Keith Leonard Haslett *(Ken's brother)*
May 2010

1942: PERSONAL DETAILS

Name:	KS HASLETT
Address:	42 Duckpool Road, Newport, Mon
Identity Card No:	XNAS III/2
Bicycle No:	767935
Size in Gloves:	6
Size in Hats:	6
Size in Boots:	2 & 3
Weight:	5 st 10 lbs Date: 1.1.42
Height:	4 ft 7 ins Date: 1.1.42

Telephone Numbers Tiverton 2335

         Totnes 3233

Name   Sgt. Haslett, Devon

         Ditto

JANUARY 1942

THURSDAY 1

Had a very nice day. Went out to play in the morning & in afternoon went to Cardiff with Mam & Sylv. Ate pie & chips (7d & very good) at Cardiff Woolworths. Caught wrong train on the way back & landed at Penarth[1] so had to catch another train <u>back</u> to Cardiff & then on to Newport. Got home safely at approx. 8.17 bought chips at Neale's[2] went home & spent a quiet evening in house.

FRIDAY 2

Had another good day. Went to Ponty[3] in morning with W. Simpson & had to wait an hour for train. Had much fun in caves etc in park. Had dinner & tea at Walter's Aunt Roses house, 14 Fountain Rd. Just managed to catch train at 3-55 pm & arrived home 4-30. Spent quiet evening in house.

SATURDAY 3

Same as other previous days. Went 2 errands for Mrs Stephens got 6d. At 11-30 A.M. went in town and spent 2/6 on quite good stamps & after dinner went back out to buy some more stamps mostly colonial coronation stamps. Spent another quiet evening in house.

SUNDAY 4

Had good day got up 8-30 am. to get tea & biscuits for Mam & Sylv. In the afternoon went to Sunday school (Hereford St Methodist) & came home 3-30. Spent another quiet evening in house.

MONDAY 5

Had rather nice day but got up rather bad tempered for Mam would not let me get up with sister who had to go to school. Went to pictures in the afternoon & came home approx 4-55 had tea & spent evening in house.

---

[1] *Apparently this mix up was explained by Mam as resulting from them asking on arrival at Cardiff station 'Is this the Newport train?'. The answer was 'Yes' because the train was FROM Newport.*

[2] *Neales fish and chip shop in Church Road.*

[3] *'Ponty' would be Pontypool. 14 Fountain Road is in Pontymoile.*

JANUARY 1942

TUESDAY 6 — Had nice day. Got up approx 9-30 stayed in house all morning. In afternoon went up yard with John Andrews & Derek Goolden. Had fights with stones which I won. Then for messing around we were sent out by Mr Andrews (John's granddad). Came home had tea & went back out to play with G.W. Dixie and played ball for a while then played about for a bit then came in at approx 7pm.

WEDNESDAY 7 — Had nice day. Got up approx 9.11am. Went over my gran's[4] for most of the morning & to pictures in afternoon. In the evening went out & had nice time came in approx. 7.40pm. Spent rest of time in house.

THURSDAY 8 — First day in school after hols. Expected to go down to 3B but happily didn't. Got up approx. 7.35. After school went out street & played till 7.30 approx then went in D. Jones house for an hour & half went home & to bed at 9.20 pm. Have cold rather bad & have very bad cough.

FRIDAY 9 — Had a nice day but eyes are very bad also have cold. Went to school & came home to spend quiet evening in house.

SATURDAY 10 — Have very bad cold. Got up approx 9.15 am had breakfast in bed. Stayed in all day doing jigsaws reading etc.

SUNDAY 11 — Got up approx 1 p.m. still have cold. Am not going to Sunday school. Have had quiet day.
P.S. done French homework

---

4. *Assume this is Gran Haslett at 42 Bristol Street.*

JANUARY 1942

MONDAY 12
Still have cold; got up approx 7.45 am. Went to school & had 2 subjects for homework. Stayed in all night. Day rather quiet.

TUESDAY 13
Still have cold. Got up 7.55 am. Went to school & had 2 subjects for homework. Went out to play & came in approx 8.0 pm.

WEDNESDAY 14
Still have cold. Got up approx 7.55 am. Went to school & had 2 subjects for homework. Spent quiet evening in house. Hope to have Atlas for my birthday but hope to have it earlier.

THURSDAY 15
Still have cold. Got up approx 7.45 am. Went to school & had 2 subjects for homework. Went out the street & came in approx 7.15 & stayed in house for the rest of the evening.

FRIDAY 16
Still have cold. Got up approx 7.45 am. Had first fall of snow today. Went to school had 3 subs for homework. Wanted to go out to play but Mam wouldn't let me. Spent quiet evening in house.

SATURDAY 17
Still have cold. Got up approx 8.15. No school today. Went out street & played on ice till dinner time. Went to see Hi Gang at the Coliseum[5] with D. Jones who went back home when we got there. Came home 7.0 pm. Spent rest of evening in house.

SUNDAY 18
Still have cold. Got up approx 11 a.m. Went to Sunday school came home and spent evening in house.
P.S. Got Mam & Sylv cup of tea in morning.

---

[5] *Cinema in Clarence Place, Newport.*

JANUARY 1942

MONDAY 19
Still have cold. Got up approx 8 am. Went to school. Came home; had 2 subjects for homework, spent evening in house.

TUESDAY 20
Still have cold. Got up approx. 7.50 am. Had a better fall of snow to-day. Went to school came home & went out street til approx 6.36 pm then done homework (2 subjects).

WEDNESDAY 21
Still have cold. Got up approx. 7.45. No snow. Went to school came home 2 subjects for homework, spent evening in house.

THURSDAY 22
Still have cold. Got up approx 7.45 am. Went to school & came home with 2 subs [KLH: subs = subjects] for homework. Went out had fun on slide at Leicester Rd. *P.S. Came home soaking wet with snow & ice.*

FRIDAY 23
Still have cold. Got up approx 7.50 went to school had 2 subs for homework. Spent evening in house.

SATURDAY 24
Still have cold but am getting better. Got up approx 8.30. Went up Aunty Phyls[6] with meat in morning and in afternoon went out town and bought some stamps. Came home and stayed in house all evening.

SUNDAY 25
Cold getting better. Got up approx 8.20 & got Mam & Sylv a cup of tea went back to bed & got up & dressed at 9.45. Went to Sunday school & after tea went to John Simpson's party & came home 8.0 pm. Spent rest of evening in house.
P.S. Also was very bad tempered & naughty & got on mam's nerves.

[6.] *'Aunty Phyl' is mam's sister Phyllis Sparkes living in Woodland Park Road: early 1950s emigrated to London, Ontario, Canada.*

JANUARY 1942

MONDAY 26   Cold better. Got up approx 7.50. Went to school & came home & had 1 subs. For homework. Spent evening in house.

TUESDAY 27   Got up approx. 7.40. Went to school came home 1 subject for homework. Went out street after tea & had fun with P. Dobele (?) my cousin who had his hat taken by sister & he came to our house telling us about it & also went to Marie Bailey's whose hat he had then his ma came so we gave the hat back.
P.S. Dobele is spelt DOBLE.

WEDNESDAY 28   Got up approx. 7.50. Went to school & came home had 2 sub for homework. Went out to play till 6.30 then spent rest of evening in house.

THURSDAY 29   Got up approx. 7.45. Went to school came home, no homework done. Went out street & had fun playing rugby, ripped pocket off old coat. Came in approx. 8.0 & spent rest of time in house. Mr Jenkins opposite Gran's tried to send us away but failed said we were to[o] noisy.

FRIDAY 30   Got up rather bad tempered at 7.40 approx. Went to school & when I came home to dinner as usual Mam said she would give us 6d a week each for chopping wood (me) & housework (sis) & that a ½d be knocked off if any arguments took place on coming back from school.
Had tea went out to play & got Mam a good deal of wood for which I got 5 maltesers then came in approx 7.50 spent rest of evening in house.

SATURDAY 31   Got up resolving to be better tempered. Got up approx 8.10. No school today. Went up Aunt Phyl's with meat & came home & washed up for Mam had gone to Mrs Boucher's to work. Went to cinema (Maindee) & saw "Ziegfeld (?) Girl" Came home had tea alone for mam had gone to get Sylv from Rona's (looks after twins every Sat). Spent evening in house & done homework.

FEBRUARY 1942

SUNDAY 1 — Got up 9.0 am & got mam a cup of tea (& Sis) & got back into bed 'til approx 10.0. Went to school (Sunday) & after school ended 3.30 played till 5.0 & then went in house to find Aunt May[7] there yapping as usual. Stayed in rest of evening.

MONDAY 2 — Still have cold. Got up approx. 7.50 am. Had a better fall of snow to-day. Went to school came home & went out strect til approx 6.36 pm then done homework (2 subjects).

TUESDAY 3 — Got up approx 7.50. Went to school came home 2 sub homework. Went out street & came in 7.45 spent rest of evening in house.

WEDNESDAY 4 — Got up approx. 7.45. Went to school came home no homework. Mam & Sis out. Went out street came home after while & spent evening in house.

THURSDAY 5 — Got up approx. 7.40. Went to school & came home 2 sub for homework. Have decided to do diary in ink & done all previous pages in pencil over. Went out street & came in 6.30 & spent rest of evening in house.

FRIDAY 6 — Got up approx 7.35. Went to school & in afternoon went to clinic to have ears done. At 4.5 went back to school for 10 mins until home time. 2 sub for homework. Spent evening in house.

SATURDAY 7 — Got up approx. 8.30. No school. Stayed in all morning & done geog homework. In afternoon went up Gran Clapp's & saw twins John & Peter[8] but didn't like it for one couldn't do anything up there. Came home & called for chips & Mam started talking to a soldier which I didn't like. Came home & spent rest of evening in house.

SUNDAY 8 — Got up approx. 8.35 to get mam a cup of tea went back to bed got up approx. 10.25 & stayed in house till I went up Aunt Phyl's with meat. Came back & had dinner went to Sunday school & decided to enter bible exam. Came home & spent rest of time in house. P.S. Happidrome ended H[arry].Korris (Mr Lovejoy) C[ecil]. Frederick (Ramsbottom) R[obbie]. Vincent (Enoch)[9].

[7.] *May Phillips: not really an aunty but the wife of Dad's mate Len Phillips who was to become Keith's godfather and from whom Keith got his middle name, Leonard.*

[8.] *Mam's nephews John and Peter Davies, sons of mam's sister Elsie and her husband Lyn.*

[9.] *A hit radio program, "Happidrome" with three North Country characters known as Mr Lovejoy, Enoch and Ramsbottom. Enoch was one of those "some mothers do have 'em" sort of characters, who eventually provoked Mr Lovejoy into (another repetitive phrase): "Take it away, Ramsbottom!" or more precisely "Tak it away!"*

FEBRUARY 1942

MONDAY 9

Got up approx. 7.55. Went to school & had 50 lines from Mr Fairclough for talking to friend J.Whitehouse who also had same. Came home 2 subs for homework. Spent evening in house. Bought lasso 81/2d at Eaton's[10] 35 ft long.

TUESDAY 10

Got up approx. 7.30. Went to school. Came home 1 sub for homework, done Physics in class. Went out & played with J.Goulden & R. Parfitt till 7.40. Came in & spent rest of evening in house.

WEDNESDAY 11

Got up approx. 7.45. Went to school & had 1 sub for homework. Pinched block of wood off Uncle Jack[11] for mam. Went out street & came in 7.40 spent rest of evening in house .
P.S. Started to do R.A.F. Jig-saw 200 pieces.

THURSDAY 12

Got up approx. 7.50. Went to school 2 sub for homework done most of it in class. Came home Mam up Nana's. Sylv has cold stayed home from school. Went out street & came in approx. 7.20. Spent rest of evening in house. Continued Jig-Saw.

FRIDAY 13

Got up approx. 7.30. Went to school 2 sb. for homework. After tea went out & played with D.Goulden, J.Goulden & R.Parfitt. But D.Goulden stopped playing for he was to[o] much of a cis but came back & played after a while. Selling some of my marbles 20 1s[12] Sold 3d to Betty Wilson & 1s to J.Goulden & also gave some to R.Riley. Went on 8.0 approx. Spent rest of time in house.
P.S. Discont. Jig-Saw.

SATURDAY 14

Got up approx. 8.45. No school. Went up Aunt Phyl's with meat but she wasn't in so I left it there. Went up rec[13] & played soccer & rugger came home 1.0. Had dinner & went up rec again with D.Jones, D&J Goulden (same before except for J Goulden) W.Simpson also came 1st time. Came home whacked at approx. 5.35. Spent rest of time in house.

SUNDAY 15

Got up approx. 8.30 to get mam a cup of tea. Went back to bed & got up approx.10.30. Pretended I was ill, therefore did not go to Sunday school. Had to lay table for tea which I did not like. Am not going in for bible exam for form had to [be] in on 18th of this month & I only see man who gave me form every Sunday. Spent quiet evening in house.

---

10. *"Eaton's" ironmongers shop on corner of Duckpool Road and Bristol Street.*
11. *Uncle Jack Faulkner, married to Dad's sister, Aunty Wyn, lived in the 'ancestral' home, 42 Bristol Street.*
12. *Can't really interpret these figures.*
13. *St Julian's Recreation Ground, later The Glebelands.*

FEBRUARY 1942

MONDAY 16   Got up approx. 7.45. Went to school & came home. 2 subs for homework. J.Whitehouse (my friend) misbehaved & had to write out theorem 6. Spent evening in house but not very peaceful being interrupted by children who wanted to buy marbles but I sold none.

TUESDAY 17   Got up approx. 7.35. Went to school & came home 3 subs for homework but done Physics. Went out street & spent it rather quietly for only 1 boy was out so came in & spent rest of evening in house.
P.S. Accidentally got ink on hand & smudged book[14].

WEDNESDAY 18   Got up approx. 7.40. Went to school & came home no homework. Went to Maindee Cinema to see "This England" Came home approx. 8.20 & spent rest of time in house.

THURSDAY 19   Got up approx. 7.40. Went to school & came home 2 subs for homework. Didn't feel like doing Chemi. so didn't do it. Went out street & had great fun over gran's back with G.W.Dixie for we climbed on Eaton's shed & started throwing things at gran's door. I then went into gran's & told Auntie Win that some boys had been in the back. Came home at 8.0 & spent rest of evening in house.

FRIDAY 20   Got up approx. 8.0. Went to school & came home 2 sub. for homework. Spent quiet evening in house reading.

SATURDAY 21   Got up approx. 8.5. No school. Went up Aunt Phyl's with meat & had 6d. Went to Maindee (Cinema) & saw "The roar of the press". Went out street & played marbles for a while with R.Parfitt but came in for it was too cold. Spent rest of time in house.
P.S. Have decided to do future entries in half French.
[KLH: see French words in *italics*]

SUNDAY 22   Got up approx. 10.20. Went *a* Sunday – *ecole et* came *chez*. Spent rest *de* time *dans chez*. Done *devoir*.

[14.] *Ken's finger- or thumb- or hand-print is an ink-stain on the page.*

FEBRUARY 1942

MONDAY 23
Got up approx. 7.40. Went *a lycee* & went up drive[15] *avec mon ami* J. Whitehouse & *je* got *un globale de glace* & brought *il chez* & put *il dans un* jar *de* jam (empty) & in afternoon went *a* find bird-nests, *mais nous* did not wish *a* take any *oeux*. 1 sub. for *devoir*. Spent quiet evening *dans chez*.

TUESDAY 24
Got up approx. 7.45. Went *a lycee* & came *chez*. *Non devoir*. Done *il dans classe*. Went out & came *dans* about 9. Spent rest *de* time (*tres* short) *dans chez*.

WEDNESDAY 25
Got up approx. 8.0. Went *a lycee* & came *chez*. 2 sub. for *devoir*. Went out street & played skipping ~~with~~ *avec* W.Simpson, G.W.Dixie, J.Simpson, D.Goulden, J.Goulden, Avril Parfitt, Hazel Brook, Jean and L.Adams, Gileon Stuart. Then with Adams, Dixie & Simpson climbed on to shelters & broke my rope. Then climbed on yard & broke record by dropping from iron bar above top of door (about 10 ft high). Came in approx. 7.30 & spent rest of time *dans chez*.

THURSDAY 26
Got up approx. 7.45. Am not going to cont. entries in Fr. Went to school 1 sub. for homework but didn't do it. Went out street & played with same kids as yesterday & came in approx. 8.0. Spent rest of time in house.

FRIDAY 27
Got up approx. 7.40. Half-day off for St David's day. Held Eistedford all morning out street all afternoon: had row with sister. Played all in rugger with M&G.Watkins (cousins), H.Goulden (who went in crying) G. Morgan & W. Simpson. M&G.Watkins & W.Simpson v me & others. We won 27-9 I scored 6 times & Morgan 2. Goulden (age 6) nearly scored but W.Simpson (14) brought him down ins from line. Got hurted & started crying.

SATURDAY 28
Got up approx. 8.30. Went out street in morning & in afternoon went up Drive with L.Adams, J & D.Goulden & W.Simpson came up after. Sent out of Drive by copper & went up Taylors Wood & were chased out by about 20 lads inc. 'bout 7 over 14. Took my rope which I bought at Eatons (81/2). Came home nearly dead. Spent quiet evening in house.

signed

[15.] *The Drive' is thought to be a short paved road from St Julian's Avenue towards the bottom end of Carlton Road. Although paved it was flanked by trees with a stream. Keith & his mates also used to use this as a jungle play area, look for birds' nests & get stung by wasps in the early 1950s.*

MARCH 1942

SUNDAY 1

Got up approx. 8.15 to get Mam & Sylv cup of biscuits[16] & went back to bed & got up approx. 9.30 & went to Sunday school & came home & spent quiet evening in house.

MONDAY 2

Got up approx. 8.30. No school half-term hols. Went to get Mrs Stephens medicine & got 6d & borrowed 3d from Mam & went to Coliseum[17] & saw "Sundown". Went out street in evening & played with D.Goulden, R.Parfitt, L.Adams & D.Jones. Came in approx 7.25 & spent rest of time in house.

TUESDAY 3

Got up approx. 7.50. Went to school & had 1 sub for homework. Stayed [in] for it was raining and played ping-pong with sister.

WEDNESDAY 4

Got up 7.45. Went to school & came home 3 sub. for homework (Arith[metic] given us by Mr.N.Fairclough our formmaster for making too much noise). Still raining so played ping-pong again with Mam & Sylv.

THURSDAY 5

Got up approx. 7.45. Went to school & had 2 sub. for homework but did not go to Chemis [?]. Went in D.Jones house & came home approx 8.45. Spent rest of time in house. *P.S. Raining.*

FRIDAY 6

Got up approx. 7.50. Went to school & had 2 subs. For homework. Had fall of snow but not a lot. Played with it in schoolyard & had fun. Mother & sis poorly. Spent quiet evening in house.

SATURDAY 7

Got up approx. 8.30. No school. In morning done errands & took rent up Rennie's. In afternoon stayed in house & in evening went out & 1st of all played chasing with D.Jones, W & J.Simpson & G.W.Dixie & R.Parfitt & chased Avril Parfitt, Iris Base, Hazel Brooks, Maggie Riley & Jean Parry only 11 & she (Jean) wanted to go with me, I refused. Then played kiss, kick or torture. Came in approx. 8.15.

SUNDAY 8

Got up early to get Mam & Sylv cup of tea & lit fire & stayed in. Went & cleaned bike & then played with a sling in garden. Went to Sunday school came home & spent quiet evening in house.

[16.] *Assume Ken meant 'cup of tea and biscuits'.*

[17.] *Cinema in Clarence Place.*

MARCH 1942

MONDAY 9

Got up approx. 7.30. Went to school & to my joy Boss said that 2nd & 3rd forms would have 2 days off while newcomers sat exam. Came home 2 sub for homework. Went out street & played with G.Dixie, D.Jones, R.Parfitt & girls namely B. Plaister, J. Harry, I.Base, A.Parfitt & J.Merret. Came in approx 7.50.

TUESDAY 10

Got up approx. 8.45. No school. No school[18]. Went to cinema & saw "Ships with Wings". Came home & went out street for a while.

WEDNESDAY 11

Got up approx 8.30. No school. Raining. Done errands for Mam & in evening Dad came home on leave & I had great fun with his pistol. Spent time & went to bed rather late at approx 10.10.
P.S. Had Nederland's badge off Dad.

THURSDAY 12

Got up approx. 7.40. Went to school & had 1 sub. for homework. Mam & Dad went out to Hereford pub[19] (done do. last night[20]). Played with Dad's pistol again. Waited up for Mam & Dad & went to bed late at approx. 11.0.

FRIDAY 13

Got up approx. 7.50. Went to school & had 3 subs. for homework. Went out for while but Mam made one go in house & therefore I lost my temper & sulked for a while & after Mam & Dad went out played with Sylv pouffet & also had cushion fight. Bought Mam birthday card. Went out street for a while but Mam made me come in for twas raining, much to my anger. Stayed up late again.

SATURDAY 14

Got up approx. 10.0. Stayed in house all morning & in afternoon all of us went out town & I had a lousy afternoon for I didn't really want to go. Came home & after tea went out street & had great fun. Came in approx. 7.30. Went to bed late again at approx 11.40.

SUNDAY 15

MAM'S BIRTHDAY

Got up about 9.30 to get cup of tea & went back up to bed with tea & got up 10.45. Went to school & came home. Spent quiet evening in house. Went to bed approx. 10.

[18.] *Ken wrote this twice, perhaps out of deep joy.*

[19.] *The 'Hereford Arms' in Hereford Street.*

[20.] *'done ditto last night', implying Mam & Dad went to the pub the night before too.*

Before entries are made below Rules 54 (June, 1937) should be carefully read, particular those paragraphs which relate to Head 11.

NEWPORT SECONDARY SCHOOL FOR BOYS

Leave these spaces blank.

No. *1809*

School.

Surname	*Hazlett*
Christian Names	*Kenneth Stanley*
Sex	
Name of Father or Guardian	*H. S. Hazlett*
Postal Address	*42 Duckpool Road*

Date of Birth		
Day	Month	Year
8	*10*	*1928*

Date of Admission		
Day	Month	Year
9	*9*	*1940*

Date of Last Attendance		
Day	Month	Year
25	*10*	*1943*

Position on Admission *Form IIc*

Position on Leaving *VB*

Boarder or Day Scholar *Day*

Taking Dept.

Form: Spring, Summer

8. Place of Residence

1. County Borough or *Newport, Mon.*

2. Borough, Urban District or Parish / County in which situate

9. Occupation of Father, or late occupation if Father is deceased or retired *Soldier*

10. Previous Education

1. Is this the first Secondary School attended (enter "yes" or "no") *Yes*

2. If so, did the pupil attend a Public Elementary School(s) in England or Wales for at least two years immediately preceding admission (enter "yes" or "no") *Yes*

3. If not, give names of all schools previously attended, whether Elementary, Secondary or other, with dates

11. Particulars of any Special Place held or of any Exemption from Tuition Fees

(a) Particulars of SPECIAL PLACE AWARD (whether carrying any remission of fees or not)

(b) Particulars of any exemption from Tuition fees other than a Special Place award

Total Exemption / Partial Exemption

(i) Granted from (Date) *Admission*

(ii) Granted by (i.e. Body financially responsible) *L.E.A.*

(iii) Extent of remission of fees. Enter "Total" "Partial" or "None" *Total*

(i) Granted from (Date)

(ii) Granted by (i.e. Body financially responsible)

(iii) If Art. 18 award enter "Art. 18"

(iv) Tenable for

12. Particulars of Public Examinations taken

Name and Date of Examination

This the pupil gain the examination as a whole. (State Yes or No.)

School Certificate or Matriculation.

Higher Certificate or Intermediate Examination for a University Degree.

13. If proceeding to an institution for full-time further education enter, in the appropriate space below, the name of the Institution.

University

University Training Dept.

Training College recognised under the Regulations for the Training of Teachers.

Secondary School.

Public Elementary School.

Any other type of full-time Institution

14. Particulars of any Scholarship or Exhibition for further education to be held elsewhere

Name of Scholarship *Junior City (Sch.)*

Name of Body awarding

13. If no entry in Head 13, state employment taken up, or how otherwise occupied

15. Remarks *Withdrawn.*

Sex	B. or D.	Status	P.E.	Father's Occup'n	Stat. Year	Age on Adm'n	Transfer in	Period of Exit	Transfer out	Sch. Cert.	Age at Leaving	Sch. Life	Occup'n	Sch'p	Hr. Cert.

Form 71 8

TOP: Ken's School Admission Form. BOTTOM LEFT: The Hereford Arms pub, Newport.
BOTTOM RIGHT: The Nederland cap badge that Ken was given by his father.

MARCH 1942

MONDAY 16   Got up approx 8.45. Went to school 1 sub. for homework. Spent evening
in house & went to bed normal time at 9.10.

TUESDAY 17   Got up approx 7.50. Went to school 2 sub. for homework. Had tea alone
for Mam Dad & Sylv had gone to cinema. Went out street for while
& had great fun. Came in approx 7.40.

WEDNESDAY 18   Got up approx 7.50. Went to school 2 sub. for homework. After tea
(in pouring rain) went up Nana Clapp's for Mam & had 3d off Aunt Elsie.
Came home had great fun with Dad & Sylv but Mam caught hold
of my braces when I was running & I fell on kettle & got burnt.
Went to bed normal time.

THURSDAY 19   Got up approx. 7.50. Went to school, no homework done it in class.
Dad gone back to unit & gave me 6d. After tea (which I had alone)
went to pictures Maindee & came home 8.30.

FRIDAY 20   Got up approx 7.50. Went to school & had 2 sub. for homework.
Went out street but came in after a while for my groin was aching.
Spent quiet evening in house.

SATURDAY 21   Got up approx. 9.30. Went a few errands & after had great fun with
sling out back. In afternoon built up old Mr.Shepherd's front garden,
the bricks of which were all about the place. In evening went out but
at 8.20 Mam made us go in so I was a bit cross but soon got over it.
*P.S. Got about 20 jam jars & took them over Mrs. Nutt's to get some
money for them[21].*

SUNDAY 22   Got up 8.15 to get Mam & Sylv cup of tea & went back to bed & got up
for good approx 9.30. Went to Sunday school & came home 3.45 & went
out street for while playing hop-scotch. Spent quiet evening in house.

[21.] *Mrs Nutt's grocery shop was on the corner of London and Manchester Streets, right next door to our
Uncle Bert and Aunty Vi's house (in Manchester Street). Shop used by our family for decades.*

MARCH 1942

MONDAY 23
Got up approx. 7.45. Went to school & have had my allotment which was 1½ – 2 perch long & ½ to ¾ perch wide.[22] (Master in charge is Mr.Hyams.) 1 sub. for homework. Went out street & had great fun. H.Brooks (fe[male?]) shut me in her house but let me out after, came in approx 8.30.

TUESDAY 24
Got up approx 7.50. Went to school & had 1 sub. for homework. Went out street & had great fun & I still hold record as best boy athlete in district. Came in late at 8.55

WEDNESDAY 25
Got up approx 7.50. Went to school. No homework. In morning messed around & in afternoon dug my garden all the time. Came home went out street for while.

THURSDAY 26
Got up approx 7.40. Went to school dug allotment all day & have now finished it. Am going to plant tomorrow or Monday. Came home very tired; no homework. Had bath when I came home. Spent quiet evening in house.

FRIDAY 27
Got up approx 7.40. Went to school. Done garden all day. 1 sub. for homework. In evening went to Olympia[23] to see "Sgt. York" with Mam & Sylv. Came home approx 8.15. Spent rest of time in house.

SATURDAY 28
Got up approx 8.10. No school. In morning went errands & in afternoon went town with Mam & Sylv to buy me shoes. After went up Nana's but I came home for I didn't want to stay there. Dined alone. Went out street & 'bashed' up D.Freebury (?). Came home approx 7.40. Spent rest of time in house.

SUNDAY 29
Got up 7.45 to get Mam & Sylv cup of tea. Went back to bed & got up for good 9.30. Done some errands. After played with sling & busted it. Had photo taken by Y.M.C.A. man. Had scrap with kid (name not known) & dislocated my 4th finger left hand, but it doesn't stop me writing. Went to Sunday school & spent quiet evening in house.

---

[22] An imperial 'perch' equals 5.0292 metres.
[23] Cinema in Skinner Street, Newport.

MARCH 1942

MONDAY 30   Got up 7.40. Went to school & for 4th day (exc. Sun. & Sat) done garden. Came home but, although had no homework, had to stay in for it was raining.

TUESDAY 31   Got up approx 7.52. Went to school, no gardening, raining. Just messed around. Came 14 in homework beat pal J.A.Whitehouse by 2 (I had average of 63) pal came 16th. Went out street & had great fun.
P.S. Scraped some of the dirt etc off old key which I found in Manchester St. some months back when navvies were digging up street. Failed to get all mess off it & put key by for later date.

signed

APRIL 1942

WEDNESDAY 1

Got up approx 7.45. Went to school for half day only for we broke up in morning for 3 weeks. In afternoon went up old warehouse by CRITERION bakery with W. Simpson & had great fun. In evening had great fun playing tag & mob. Came in approx 8.15.

THURSDAY 2

Got up 8.0. In morning done errands & in afternoon went out Somerton to play on tumps etc with D. Jones, G.W. Dixey & J & D. Goulding. D.J.,G.W.D. & D.G. went home early but J.G. & I stayed & on way home saw convoy of 40 odd light & heavy armoured cars. Had hot-cross buns (home made) for tea. After tea went out street & played hop-scotch & mob with ner[24] all minus 3 of all boys & girls in London Street.

FRIDAY 3

Got up approx. 8.40. In morning went out street & in afternoon went out again to play hop-scotch for while then with W. Simpson, L.Adams[25] & R. Parfitt. R.P. & me fought others which we won (fought up ware-house). L.A. copped a heavy stone (fired by me) on his head above his right eye the bruise being tremendous size at least 1.5 inches across. Came in spent a quiet evening in house for twas raining. *P.S. Had R.A.F. badge of W. Simpson. Had air-raid in night starting approx 10.50 & lasting for about 20 minutes.*

SATURDAY 4

Got up approx 8.20. Had alert begin rung 8.45 lasted 5 mins. In morning went to King's in Prince Street[26] for Mam & after played hop-scotch. In afternoon went to cinema with Mam to see "City for Conquest" with J. Cagney. Had alert while in cinema, started 4.45 lasting 5 mins. Spent quiet evening in house. *P.S. Big Ben struck 10 instead of 9 to warn people to put clocks on 1 hr.*

SUNDAY 5

Got up 9.10 to get Mam & Sylv cup of tea. Got up for good approx 9.45. In morning done errands & in afternoon went to school & it being open Mam, Mrs & Nora Stephens came. Had vocal & recitations by Mde. N. Garbett, Miss J. Jewel, Master C. Sansom, Mr F. Church & Farrington (?) that latter living in Annesley Road. In evening went to play in spare room & had row with Sylv. Had air raid alert beginning 5.45 & lasting about 10 mins. Spent evening in house. Cleaned souvenirs of war for have box.

---

[24] *Couldn't decipher this any better.*

[25] *L. (Les) Adams has had several mentions in this diary. By a strange coincidence he became loosely related to the family when his daughter Caroline married Mark Abraham, Keith's brother-in-law. In later life Les became victim to a series of benign brain tumours. Ken was heard to express the hope that these were not a result of the above incident on Friday April 3rd, 1942. Any such causal effect was never scientifically proved.*

[26] *King's in Prince Street was a timber yard, a good source of free offcuts for kindling and free sawdust for pet bedding.*

APRIL 1942

MONDAY 6

Got up 9.10. In morning went up the Bakers Yard with W. Simpson & R.Parfitt & had great fun. After dinner tried to get in cinema but couldn't get in anywhere, so, much to my disgust (with Mam & Sylv) went up Nana Clapp's & stayed for tea. Had lousy time up there came home, very tired approx 9.40.
P.S. Auntie Elsie gave me 3d.

TUESDAY 7

Got up approx. 8.20. Done a few errands for Mam but couldn't go out to play for it was raining. In afternoon went to cinema with Mam & Sylv to see "Tugboat Annie Sails Again". Came home went out street for while & had great fun. Came in approx 8.0.

WEDNESDAY 8

Got up approx. 8.30. Went out to Woolworths to buy seeds for garden. In afternoon played hop-scotch (of which I am still champion) & after tea went up Bakers Yard & fought 6 v me & through clever moves on my part managed (unseen) to get on top of shed forcing them to surrender. Came in 8.15. Had bath.

THURSDAY 9

Got up approx 9.30. Have very bad cold. Mam brought me home a leather belt off Mr. Pickman of "Yvonne" Carlton Road. Have 40 odd pieces of shrapnel, fins of incendiary bomb & 3 pieces (large) of Nazi Bomber & several badges etc. Stayed in all morning & afternoon. In evening went out street, played with D. Freebury, W. Simpson, L. Adams, D. Hill. One of them (& J. Morgan) threw stone at me & as he wouldn't own up I hit all of them. Came in 8 for it was raining.

FRIDAY 10

Got up approx. 9.15. Stayed in all morning for have bad cold also 'blind' boil up my nose. In afternoon went to cinema with Mam & Sylv to see "Yes, Madam" & "Flight from Destiny". Came home & after tea went out street & played spy game with (girls) A. Parfitt, J. Merrett (?), S. Base (Boys) D & J Goulding, R. Parfitt & me. Played good game of spies. Came in 8.55.

SATURDAY 11

Got up approx 9.30. Cold little better & had breakfast in bed. In morning stayed in & in afternoon went out market on bus with R. Parfitt to buy 3/- of chicks & some chick food but failed. Saw Hindu who told Horoscope for 1/- or 1d. In evening played spies with same as yesterday minus D. Goulding & plus D. Jones, G.W. Dixey & Betty Plaister; J. Morgan. Came in 8.5.

APRIL 1942

SUNDAY 12
Got up 8.5. to get Mam & Sylv cup of tea. Got up for good 9.40.
Lighted fire & to peel "spuds". After took a very heavy fire-guard to Albert
Terrace (Nana Clapp's) & had 1/- of Aunt Elsie. Went to school.
Aunt Elsie & her twins (age nearly 1) came to tea. In evening went
out street (always go to London & Bristol Street to play).
P.S. Am wearing open shirt.

MONDAY 13
Got up 8.30. Sylv had to go to school. In morning went to King's for wood
for Mrs Stephens & Mrs Haines. Had 6d off both people, & after went
to collect salvage with J. Goulding & R. Parfitt. Collected half cwt had
4d each. In afternoon went up baths & swum several lengths. After had
scrap with kid (name unknown) & blacked his eye & made his nose bleed.
Went out street & had great fun. (Bashed up J. Norval).

TUESDAY 14
Got up approx. 8.30. Went few errands & went to play til dinner.
In afternoon went up allotment & planted peas, Potatoes, Turnips
& Radish. Came home 5.5. In evening went out street & had great fun.

WEDNESDAY 15
Got up 8.35. In morning went out street for while & after dug up our
lawn for Mam to plant seeds in. In afternoon went up garden & found
parsley coming through. Planted only for a while, doing only onions,
having no room for my lettuce. Watched cricket XI practising under Mr.
Fairclough. In evening went to cinema to see "The Phantom Light".

THURSDAY 16
Got up 7.55. In morning went to play, afternoon ditto. In evening went
out street again & had great fun. Am learning backslang but am not
bothering much about it.
*P.S. In morning went salvage collecting with J. Goulding & collected
half cwt[27] & got 6d each.*

FRIDAY 17
Got up 8.20. In morning went out street. In afternoon went to see Mrs
Allan's funeral, but went to see 2 Bren Gun carriers with E. Morgan
& saw new rifles & new 6 inch bayonet. Also with E.M. & G.W. Dixey
had ride in 1 of the B.G.C's. In evening with L. Adams, D. Goulding,
& R. Parfitt went up rec & had great fun. Had fight with (mock) a half-wit
& man named "Ernie". Came home 8.27. Spent rest of time in house.

---

[27] *1 cwt = 112 lbs or approximately 50 kilograms*

APRIL 1942

SATURDAY 18

Got up approx 8.0. In morning washed up done errands & got wood from King's for Mam. In afternoon played with R & A Parfitt & L. Adams. Had air raid NIGHT BEFORE LAST at 3.0am & lasting 10 mins. In evening went to cinema to see "Magic & Music" & "Rivers End". Came home 8.50.

SUNDAY 19

Got up 8.5. to get Mam & Sylv cup of tea, got up for good 9.45. In morning stayed in & in afternoon went to school. In evening went out street for while but came in 6.40. Wrote letter to Dad.
Heard cuckoo.
In April the cuckoo shows his bill
In May he sings all day
In June he sings a different tune.

MONDAY 20

Got up 8.15. In morning done errands, boys in school. In afternoon went up rec with L. Adams & R. Parfitt & had great fun. Buried (partly) "Ernie" with grass while he was sleeping. In evening had great fun up Bakery fighting with stones. G.W. Dixey hit me on ankle (hard) but I returned fire & cut his face by his mouth. Also blacked G. Harry's eye. Came in 8.50.

TUESDAY 21

Got up early & chopped wood for Mam. All morning done errands for Mam & also washed up. In afternoon went out street for while but no one out so stayed in. Mam up Nana Clapp's so had tea with Sylv. In evening went out street & had great fun.
Bought pads & 5H pencil totalling ¼ for school.

WEDNESDAY 22

Got up 7.40. First day in school. Head (Atkinson) appointed 6 more prefects therefore making no. up to 13. No homework. Went out to play & for 3rd day running had loan of tennis racquet off Mrs Hawksley (?) of 28 Bristol Street, Came in 8.40.

THURSDAY 23

Got up 7.50. Went to school. Name of prefects disclosed. R. Diaper, K. James, C. Butcher, Bartlett, Forbes, Leith. 1 sub. for homework. Went to cinema to see "Hoppity goes to town". My eyes are getting sore so am going up clinic to have glasses changed. Came home approx 8.30.

APRIL 1942

FRIDAY 24

Got up 7.50. Went to school, 3 sub. for homework. In evening went out street & had great fun playing with (males) D. Jones, G.W. Dixey, R. Parfitt (females) E. Jones, J. Stevens, B. Wilson & sister. Came in 9.10.

SATURDAY 25

Got up 8.35. No school. In morning (boys being in school) had great fun on Gran's shed & pulling Aunt Win's leg etc. In afternoon ditto. In evening went out street & after resting for a while for it was boiling hot played cricket & knocked ball clean through Mrs Stuart's open window. Got another ball which went over Mrs Owen's back but I jumped over wall to get it & succeeded. Came in 8.10.

SUNDAY 26

Got up 9.50. Sylv got cup of tea. I was asleep. 2 alerts. 10.30 – 12.10 & 4.45 – 6.0am. Slight activity. In morning chopped wood for Mam. Could not go to Sunday school for Mam & me could not get any trousers for me. Went out back in sun. For nearly a year have wished I was older to do something to help war effort. Want to join Army. Spent quiet evening in house.

MONDAY 27

Got up 8.0. Went to school. No homework. In evening out street & had great fun.

TUESDAY 28

Got up 8.5. Went to school. 1 sub for homework. Done homework & then played mob out street in shelters. Played with R. Parfitt, K & D. Goulding, M. Riley & H. Brooke. Came in 9.5.

WEDNESDAY 29

Got up 8.0. Went to school & S. Mcall (?) Prefect who told me to stay in which I didn't. 2 sub. for homework stayed in all night to do homework well. Have to use different pen as my pen has been broken.

THURSDAY 30

Got up 8.0. Went to school & had 1 sub. for homework. In evening went out street & had great fun playing mob & tag. Played mob in shelters at bottom of London Street & Joyce Palmer smashed lamp & D. Goulding & I went up Bakery & smashed windows & knocked supports of window. Thought copper in Mrs Walsh's caught us, didn't.

MAY 1942

FRIDAY 1

Got up 7.40. Went to school & after school went up garden & found to my joy, my Peas, Radish, are coming & onions also. 2 sub. for home work. Went out street but stayed out til 9.15 & Mam had to fetch me & Sylv. Had inflammation in stomach.

SATURDAY 2

Got up 8.30. In morning done errands. In afternoon went out street & had 2 bots. of pop. In evening went out street & came in 8.40. For had headache.

SUNDAY 3

Got up early to get Mam & Sylv cup of tea. Got up for good 9.15. In morning D. Jones & W. Simpson. Went 1.5 miles out of course left W.W. miles behind. D.J. & me got home 6.45. Did not got into Barry too tired, but W.S. did & got home 7.45. Spent evening in house.[28] End of Hi Gang! on Radio. Bebe, Vic & Ben[29].

MONDAY 4

Got up 8.0. Went school. I sub. for homework. Went up allotment & partly watered garden. Sun out to[o] much to water. Went out street & had great fun.

TUESDAY 5

Got up 8.0. Went to school & in afternoon went up clinic with Mam to see about eyes. I sub. for homework. Went out street & played rugger out street with J.S., D. Goulding & R.Parfitt & D.G. & me won 12-3. Came in 8.10.

WEDNESDAY 6

Got up 7.30. Had breakfast early to go & water garden before sun came out, with A. Whitehouse. Mr. Fairclough is back again. 2 subs. for home-work. R. Riley, K. Goulding & E. Lewis have bust nearly every window up the BAKER'S yard. Had great fun playing mob in shelters with R. Parfitt, G.W. Dixey & R. Heard. Had book of [f] Gran called "Standard ready reckoner". Aunt Elsie & twins at our house to tea.

THURSDAY 7

Got up 7.50. Went to school for a while & at 9.30 had to go up clinic about my eyes. Dr. Robinson said they were worst & have to have them changed & wear them all time. Came out of clinic approx 11.0. Did not go to school in morning or in afternoon. Went out street in evening & had great fun.

[28.] *This is a day of strangely recorded activity that makes little immediate sense.*

[29.] *Bebe Daniels, Vic Oliver & Ben Lyon.*

MAY 1942

FRIDAY 8

Got up 8.0. Went school. 1 sub. for homework. Eyes still bad, have not having my glasses back til Monday. Bought cricket ball, went up rec. Scored 26 runs. Came home 9.10.

SATURDAY 9

Got up 8.45. No school. In morning done errands & in afternoon went up "Brickies"[30] with W & J. Simpson, D. Jones, I. Bowman[31], D. Hill & R. Parfitt. Also went up after tea with R. Parfitt & D. Jones & 3 girls namely M. Haines & J & Y. Stevens. Came home 8.15.

SUNDAY 10

Got up 8.30 to get Mam & Sylv tea & biscuits. Went back to bed got up for good approx 10.5. Done errand for Mrs. Hancock & had 1.5d off her. Camouflaged myself out back with leaves etc. Went to school. Came home & spent quiet evening in house.
P.S. Rain at last for gardens.

MONDAY 11

Got up 8.0. Went to school. 1 sub. for homework. Have had glasses back from Hudson Howards. Have cleaned up my sword & found inscription reads (roughly) Pro Deo A (?) Patrice. Went out street for while & came in approx 5.40. E. Smalldon at 38 Duckpool Rd helped me do my homework.

TUESDAY 12

Got up 7.55. Went school 2 subs for homework. Have stye or abscess in eye & Mam took me up clinic for she thought it might be my glasses. Did not go out street for it was raining again. Hung maps of Guernsey, Jersey & St. Malo & Cherbourg which I bought off H. Rudge for 3d.

WEDNESDAY 13

Got up 8.0. Went to school & had 2 subs. for homework. Wisp still there on my eye. Went out street & had game of mob. Came in for it was raining at approx 7.40.

THURSDAY 14

Got up 7.45. Went school & had 2 subs. for homework. Aunt Elsie & twins John & Peter were at our house for tea. Went up clinic about eye. Aunt Elsie went home 9.25. I went out street & had great fun playing rounders & after with G. Morgan went round Ash-Corts to where Raid Shelters are & had great fun jumping off a bus onto sand below.

[30.] *This could be the Brickyard Pond, a drowned quarry, off Caerleon Road, now filled in and overtopped by the M4 as it approaches the Usk and the Brynglas tunnels.*

[31.] *Ken famously had a chipped front tooth. I.(Ivor) Bowman proudly admitted to being the one who did it.*

MAY 1942

FRIDAY 15

Got up 7.40. Went school 3 sub. for homework. Went up allotment
to weed. Had some sprouts, cabbage & lettuce to transplant of M. Lee
& B. Edwards. W.E. Edwards is leaving after Whitsun. Raining, came
home at 6.5 with E. Bullock. Did not go out, raining.
*Had party over Gran's. Uncle Charlie home from London to go to his
son's (Stanley's) wedding to Gwyneth Griffiths.*

SATURDAY 16

Got up early with Sylve to get Mam cup of tea, for she was ill last night.
Done errands in morning. Still have wisp. In afternoon went to cinema
with W. Simpson to see 'Strawberry Blonde' with James Cagney.
In evening went out street & fell and buckled glasses & cut face in
5 different places. Came in 8.30.

SUNDAY 17

Got up early to get Mam & Sylv cup of tea. Got up for good 10.35.
Stayed in all morning except when I went over Gran's. Gran may teach
me to play accordion[32]. Sores on face very painful. Mam put some zinc
on them. Still have stye which is a lot better. Did not go to school.
Done homework. Aunt Elsie is going to take my glasses to Hudson
Howards to be mended. Stayed in all evening.

MONDAY 18

Got up 8.0. Went to school & had no homework. Could not go out street
for it was raining so stayed in & drew.
P.S. Stanley married today[33].

TUESDAY 19

Got up 7.50. Went to school & had 1 sub. for homework. Had not had
any maths homework since Monday for Mr. Fairclough is absent.
Went out street & played ON shelters in Liverpool Street with L. Roberts,
S. Dougan, W. Rackam (?), R. Wilson & D. Short. Had great fun.

WEDNESDAY 20

Got up 7.30. Went to school & in afternoon with rest of school went
to school cricket grounds to see 1st match ever played on school grounds
v[ersus] 5-Ways. Drew. After went up allotment to transplant lettuce
& plant spuds. 1 sub for homework. Went round to play with sand again.
Came in 8.25.

---

[32] *This was not a full size accordion but a cutdown version out of which Gran could apparently get a fair
tune. After her death this instrument ended up at 42 Duckpool Road, getting tattier.*

[33] *Cousin Stanley Haslett, son of Uncle Charlie, Horace's oldest brother*

MAY 1942

THURSDAY 21   Got up 8.5. Went to school. Face healed. Went up allotments. Aunt Elsie & twins (Peter Quentin & John Evan) came out to tea. Went out street & played same place as before. Came in 10.5 (very late).

FRIDAY 22   Got up 7.0 to go up & water allotment. Cooked own breakfast of Bacon & Potatoes & Fried Bread. 1 sub. for homework. No school in afternoon, half holiday for Empire Day (Sunday) also Monday & Tuesday off for Whitsun. In afternoon went out town with Mam & Sylv. Mam bought me new school blazer which I wanted & a pair of crepe soled shoes. After went up Gran Clapp's. Came home approx 8.10. Had glasses back, cost 2/6d.

SATURDAY 23   Got up 9.30. Done errands all morning. In afternoon went out street & had great fun with R. Parfitt, I. Bowman & D. Goulding. Hit J. Goulding for messing around. Broke glasses again. Have to have a new arm put on cost 3/6d. Having them back tonight. In evening got glasses back & went up Aunt Phyl's with her order for she is ill. Got 1/2d off her & Uncle. Have now got 2/- & Mam is giving me 6d, already gave me 3d.

SUNDAY 24   Got up 9.25. Went to Sunday School in morning afternoon & evening. Sylv & M. Bailey sang, singing "Jerusalem" (Satanic Mills). Mam, Nora & Mrs Stephens came in afternoon & Mam & Nora in evening. Other children also sang. Am having Whitsun Treat tomorrow.

MONDAY 25   Got up 8.50. Went to Sunday School 10.15 & at 11.0 went up with school to Summerhill Avenue church. Came home 12.0. In afternoon stayed in house & at 4.0 went to Church Road School & had tea. I ate 6 pieces of cake, 4 rounds of bread & MARG & 3 cups of tea. After had great fun. Came home 7.5.

TUESDAY 26   Got up 8.45. In morning played cricket [?] with Sylv. In afternoon went to cinema (Olympia) with Sylv to see "South American George" with G. Formby. Came home 5.0. In evening done homework & after went out street & had great fun playing with G.W. Dixey & girls. M. Bailey, Sister & M. Gilbert. Came in 8.50.

MAY 1942

WEDNESDAY 27   Got up 8.0. School. 2 sub. for homework. Had row with Sylv. Went out street & had great fun. Came in 8.15.

THURSDAY 28   Got up 8.0. Went to school & in evening after school went allotments. Got caught in storm on way home & came in drenched. Did not go out, raining.

FRIDAY 29   Got up 7.40. Went to school. Had 2 free periods for Mr. E.G. Thomas is at camp with the A.I.C[34]. Had 2 sub. for homework. In evening went out street & had GREAT fun playing with Sylv, Marie Gilbert & R. Parfitt & Avril Parfitt (?) & I. Bowman. Came in 7.50. *P.S. Had bath.*

SATURDAY 30   Got up 8.45. Done errands in morning. In afternoon W. Simpson threw 5d away & I got 4d. Some kids hit D. Goulding in Merriots Place & J. Goulding & me went round fought 3 to 1 & beat them. At 7.30 went up Nana Clapp's to get Sylv. Went out street for while after. Came in 8.43.

SUNDAY 31   Got up to get Mam & Sylv cup of tea. Got up for good 9.20. In morning went up Aunt Phyl's for mam & had 6d off her. Heard Mr & Mrs Jones fighting 3 times next door. Went to school. Stayed out back all night & had great fun by myself. Also for 5 min played soccer with Mam. *P.S. I went to Marie Bailey's party.*

---

[34] *A.I.C.: Army Intelligence Corps?*

JUNE 1942

MONDAY 1
Got up 7.50. Mr. Fairclough & Mr. E.G. Thomas are back. Went to school & had 2 sub. for homework. For last 2 periods in afternoon played cricket v[ersus] 3L & I opened innings scored 2 runs then bowled by Fleet. Had great fun about back in evening. Came in 8.45. Bought 5H pencil, lost previous one.

TUESDAY 2
Got up 7.50. Went to school & had 2 subs. for homework. In evening at 7.0 went up Mr. Parfitt's allotment by rec with son Ray. Had game of cricket for half hour & scored 8 runs 'fore being bowled by E.G. Thomas[35]. Very hot weather. Done a lot of work up allotment & came home tired at 9.45. One of Uncle Jack's 2 doe rabbits dead. 6 weeks old.

WEDNESDAY 3
Got up 7.10. Went to school & had 3 sub for homework. Aunt Elsie & twins down to tea. On way to Nana Clapp's with Aunt Elsie & twins & Mam & Sylv saw barrage balloon under railway bridge on River Usk. Got home late hour of 11.30. "Bunny" Austin IVL registered temperature 104 degrees. Tar up on Caerleon & Chepstow Rd[36].

THURSDAY 4
Got up 7.45. Went to school & had 2 subs. for homework. Went out street & at 6.45 went up Nana Clapp's for Mam. Bought bottle of "Tizer" for myself. "Bunny" Austin registered temperature in morning (11.30) to be 105 degrees & at 2.0 115 degrees. Played marbles & won 11. B.V. Edwards IIIA (my form) gave me kitten. Came in 8.45.

FRIDAY 5
Got up 7.45. Went to school & had 3 subs. for homework. K. James prefect made me go on late line. Tiddles our old cat is going to be destroyed for he is 10 & a half years old. Went out back to catch butterflies: caught 3. R. Parfitt who was catching them caught 1. Had bath.

SATURDAY 6
Got up 8.30. No school. Done few errands for Mam. Went up Gran Clapp's to get Sylv from there. Saw twins. Came home 9.0. Tiddles destroyed today. I am very sorry & shed a few tears. May go to Bullmore or Barry tomorrow.

---

[35] Not the teacher E.G. Thomas but a boy indicated by Ken as being a pupil at his school in, I think, class U1A ?

[36] On very hot summer days, even in 1950's, road tar used to bubble up.

JUNE 1942

SUNDAY 7   Got Mam & Sylv cup of tea. Went to Bullmore[37] with Mam & Sylv,
D. Jones & Jean & Yvonne Stevens. Had great fun out there.
Got sunburnt rather badly. Came home 6.35. Spent rest of time in house.

MONDAY 8   Got up 7.45. Went to school & had 2 sub. for homework. In evening went
out back for while & had great fun. Went up plot to weed.
Came in from back 8.30.

TUESDAY 9   Got up 8.0. Went to school. No homework. Mr. Long absent
& Mr. Fairclough forgot to give it us. Inspection of plots by Headmaster
(Boss) & "Cocky" Hyams. Had cricket in afternoon. No runs.
Bowled by Mr. Fairclough. Went up rec in evening to play cricket again.
Scored 2 runs. Came home 9.0.

WEDNESDAY 10   Got [up] 7.50. Went to school & had 2 sub. for homework.
Went out street for while & after went in T. Riley's house to help him
build rabbit hutch. Uncle Jack's other doe rabbit dead. Came in 7.40.

THURSDAY 11   Got up 7.55. Went to school & had 2 sub. for homework. K. James put
me on late line again also Mr. D.H. Jones gave me detention.
Did detention. Am going on late line tomorrow. Played cricket
out back with Sylv. Dad coming home either 9.0. tonight
or 1.0 tomorrow morning.

FRIDAY 12   Got up 7.45. Went to school & had 3 sub. for homework.
Dad came home 9.0 yesterday. He brought Mam diamond ring
& I had a lovely "Ensign" folding camera. Stayed in all night with Sylv.
Mam & Dad went out so Sylv & I stayed up for them. Bed late 10.45.

SATURDAY 13   Got up 9.30. No school. W. Simpson got an old rifle like G[ary] Cooper's
in "Sgt. York" with inscription D EGG on it. The cocking piece keeps
falling off. He came out our back yesterday & we had great fun.
Went bed late.
P.S. In afternoon went to cinema with W. Simpson to see "Corsican Brothers".

[37.] *Bullmore Lido near the Old Village, Caerleon.*

JUNE 1942

SUNDAY 14   Got up early got Mam & Sylv cup of tea. Stayed in morning & done homework. In afternoon went to school in evening played cards with Dad, Sylv & Mam & won 3d. Stayed in all evening.

MONDAY 15   Got up 7.55. Went to school & had 1 sub. for homework.
In evening had great fun out back playing cricket with Sylv.
Mam & Dad went out for night. Came home 10.45. Late bed.
P.S. Went to cinema to see "Ball of Fire".

TUESDAY 16   Got up 7.59. Went to school & had 2 sub. for homework. Mam & Dad out again. Went out back by myself & had great fun. Went bed 10.15.

WEDNESDAY 17   Got up 8.0. Went to school. Very tired. 2 sub. for homework.
Went out street & had great fun. Went to bed 10.45.

THURSDAY 18   Got up 7.45. Went to school. Very tired. 1 sub. for homework.
S. McAll prefect put me on late line but I am going on tomorrow.
Went to Vine Place, played cricket with W. Pope, G. Morgan, J.M. Cook, A. Parker & G & M. Watkins. I scored 133 runs in 1 innings & got them all out in 8 bowls. Came in 9.30. Had party in house. Fight outside our house with 2 Q.C. Sgts & Sappers[38]. Went to bed 1.30 AM.

FRIDAY 19   Got up 10.15. Did not go to school in morning. Dad is going back today.
3 sub. for homework. Went in late line & Leith prefect is going to give me a detention for messing about. With Mam & Sylv went to cinema to see "Babes on Broadway". Mam payed. Came home 8.55.
Got fish & chips from Neale's.

SATURDAY 20   Got up 10.0. No school. Done errands in morning & went out street in afternoon. In evening played cricket up Bakers yard & after climbed up roof to unlock door of loft. Succeeded but could not open door.
Came in 8.50.

[38.] *This could be the time that Ken told of where Dad donned his NCO's tunic and went outside to break up the fight, bringing the two combatants into the house to clean themselves up.*

JUNE 1942

SUNDAY 21 — Got Mam & Sylv cup of tea. Up for good 9.30. Went to Lighthouse with D. Jones, W. Simpson, G. Harris, W. Gail (?) & W. Morgan. I found some teeth set in a jaw & various coloured stones & a fossil of a crustacean. Came home 8.0.

MONDAY 22 — No school. Half term hols. Got up 7.30. In morning done errands & in afternoon went to see "Weekend in Havana". Played cricket & lost ball.

TUESDAY 23 — Got up 7.40. Went to school & had 1 sub. for homework. Went out & played cricket up Bakers Yard. In 8.30.

WEDNESDAY 24 — Got up 8.0. Went to school & had 2 subs. for homework. Aunt Elsie & twins here for tea. Sylv, Mam & me went up park with them after had chips at Eveswell Fish Bar. Home 9.15 – 25.

THURSDAY 25 — Got up 7.45. Went to school & had 2 sub. for homework. No baths for Mr. Tregurtha is ill. Cricket in afternoon. I scored 1 run & caught 1 out. Went up Beechwood Park & played cricket with M & R. Dyke, J.M. Cook & boys named Poole (?) & Whitfield. Former goes to IV (S.J.) H.S. & is in IIB. Came home 7.10.
P.S. Got 2 out bowled.

FRIDAY 26 — Got up 7.45. Went to school & 3 sub. for homework. Went up allotment & done a lot of weeding. Had cabbage off B.V. Edwards. Stayed in all night.

SATURDAY 27 — Got up 8.30. No school. Bought Middle-East war map & done errands. In evening with little R. Riley I found 3 balls: 2 on ledge above big doors at Bakers Yard & other in street. Came in 8.25.

Photo credit: the Doble family

Photo credit: Newportpast.com

TOP: The Brickyard Pond, Newport. Visited by Ken on 9th May 1942.
BOTTOM: German aerial image of Alexandra Dock, Newport.

JUNE 1942

SUNDAY 28 Got up 12.30. I am ill. I have bad glands & wisp or stye in my eye. Had breakfast in bed. Did not go to Sunday School & ate no dinner. Bed 10.10.

MONDAY 29 Got up 7.45. School. 1 sub. for homework. Went up rec. with Torrington (?) IIIB & P. Hourahine IIIB & W. (?) Alexander IIIB, Watkins IIIB. Scored 8 runs & got 4 boys out (all bowled). Home 8.15. Am not so ill. Aunt Elsie & twins to dinner & tea.
P.S. Me & Sylv had 6d each of Aunt Elsie.

TUESDAY 30 Got up 7.45. School. 2 sub for homework. I am having J. Constable's allotment. I have now 2 and a half plots & J. Whitehouse 1 and a half. Allotments in evening. Stayed in all night.

JULY 1942

WEDNESDAY 1 — Got up 7.30. School. 2 sub for homework. Up allotment & Beechwood Park to play cricket. I scored 10 runs. Bowled 3 boys & caught 2. Stayed in rest of time & was home 8.30 approx.

THURSDAY 2 — Got up 8.25. School. 1 sub. for homework. School's (N[S.J.] H.S.) 1st anniversary today. In evening went up rec with Torrington & Co. I bowled 1 out & caught 2 off own bowls. Came home. 8.40. approx.

FRIDAY 3 — Got up 8.0. School. No homework. No cricket, ground dangerous. Went up allotment. Planted 22 lettuces in new plot purchased off T. Joseph & R. Nicholas. Raining today. I took home 1 lettuce, 3 turnips & a big bunch of parsley. Stayed in all evening.

SATURDAY 4 — Got up 9.0 approx. No school. In morning done errands & broke 1 of our windows & making my record of breaking windows to NINE (incl. 3 of ours). In afternoon went to cinema to see "Hot Spot". In evening went out street & played Spanish Fly. In 8.40.

SUNDAY 5 — Got up 8.50. In morning helped Mam & in afternoon went to school. Went out street for while in evening. In 8.20.

MONDAY 6 — Got up 7.45. Went to school. 1 sub for homework. Stayed in all day. *P.S. It is raining today. Went up plots for while.*

TUESDAY 7 — Got [up] 7.55. Went to school. No homework. Swotted for exam. Went up plot again. Swotted all night for exam. Raining.

JULY 1942

WEDNESDAY 8   Got up 7.55. Went to school. No homework. Went up plot to plant onions & cabbage. Swotted. Exam tomorrow. Went out street for while & had great fun. In 9.5.

THURSDAY 9   Got up 7.50. School. No homework. Exam today. English & Geography. Did not do so badly I think. Went in R. Parfitt's house for while. W. Simpson gave me 2 stamps & a picture & diary of Prof. Picard's ascent into the stratosphere 1931 which to my horror I LOST. In 8.40 approx.

FRIDAY 10   Got up 8.10. School. Exams again. Algebra (at which I am lit. lousy) & Physics. No homework. Swotting. In evening went out street & caught 8 & bowled 17 wickets belonging to boys, ages varying from 10 – 13 & I scored 33 runs. This proves I am better at bowling than batting. Came in 9.5.

SATURDAY 11   Got up 8.50. No school. In morning went up rec. with D. Freebury (?), K. Fleet & E. Morgan. I bowled K.F. & caught D.F. D.F. bowled E.M. I scored 50 runs & retired. Went in W. Simpson's house in afternoon. In evening played cricket. Ages same as yesterday. Got out in 7 innings 28 & made 83 runs.

SUNDAY 12   Got up early to get Mam & Sylv cup of tea. Went up Aunt Phyl's. Peter one of the twins had abscess under chin & has to go in hospital. Went to school. Stayed in all night.

MONDAY 13   Got [up] 7.50. School. Chem & History exam. In evening went out street scored 57 runs & got 23 out. In 9.0.

TUESDAY 14   Got up 7.50. School. Exam Geometry & Arithmetic. No homework. Went out street to play cricket. 25 out 53 runs. In 9.5. 21 off own bowled 4 off other bowls. Played with I. Bowman, J. Goulding, E. Morgan, boy named Gwyn P..? & G. W. Dixey & R. Parfitt. Raining off & on. Am going to do future entries in part French. [KLH: again, see French words in *italics*]

JULY 1942

WEDNESDAY 15

Got up 8.5. *Lycee.* Exam. *Francais dans matin. Non devoir.* Went up rec. *a* play cricket. *Dans trois* innings scored 34 runs got 4 out. *Chez* 8.30.

THURSDAY 16

Got up 7.40. *Lycee.* Art *dans matin. Non devoir.* Went *a cinema voir* "Sante Fe Trail". *Dans* 8.5. Stayed *dans* rest *d'heure.* Raining *sur et* off.

FRIDAY 17

Got up 7.50. *Lycee.* Woodwork theory. *Non devoir.* Went out *rue et* played crickct. 21 runs 8 out. In 8.45.
P.S. Brought from plot un grand *cabbage,* trois grand *lettuce, peas, quarter beetroot.*

SATURDAY 18

Got up 8.5. *Non lycee.* Done errands *dans matin et dans* afternoon went *voir "Un de notre* aircraft *est* missing" at cinema. Played mob *dans soir. Dans* 9.0 exactly.

SUNDAY 19

Got up early *obtainer maman et soeur* cup *de* tea, *Dans après midi* went *a* Sunday *ecole.* Went out *rue dans soir et* had *un livre de* jiu-jitsu *de* W. Simpson. Came *chez* 8.40.
P.S. Have now un *considerable supply of biscuits* dans ma salle.

MONDAY 20

Got up after tea for *je suis malade. As* diarrhea & *suis* sick. Did *n'aller pas lycee.* Stayed *chez tous jour.*

TUESDAY 21

Got up 11.43. Am very much better. Did not go to school, but, as I felt very much better went out street to play & had record night for bowling taking 32 wickets & making 112 runs. In 9.5.

JULY 1942

WEDNESDAY 22   Got up 8.10. School. No homework. In dinner hour went plot to pick
6 big lettuce, giving 1 to Gran, 1 to Mrs. Williams for loan of tools,
1 to Mrs Stephens for 3d. We have the fuselage of a Curtiss Hawk fighter
up our school for A.I.C. In evening went with Mam & Sylv to cinema
to see "Roar the Wild Wind". In 8.25.

THURSDAY 23   Got up 7.50. School. No homework. Went out street to play cricket.
In 5 innings got 23 out & scored 50 runs. In 9.15.

FRIDAY 24   Got up 7.45. School. No homework. Went up rec. with some 2nd formers
v[ersus] 1st form Brynglas. In 2 innings I got 3 out & made 2 runs
(only 5 on each side). We won easily. In 8.5.approx.
P.S. Peter one of twins is out of hospital.

SATURDAY 25   Got up 8.25. No school. Went up baths in morning with J. Cousins,
P. McIntosh & D. Barnes. In afternoon went up rec. to play cricket.
7 out 42 runs (2 innings). In evening went to field on River Usk bank
to play cricket. In 3 innings (2 no runs to be scored) got 5 out & 7 runs.
Home 9.15.

SUNDAY 26   Got up early to get Mam & Sylv cup of tea. Went up Gran Clapp's
& had 3d off her. Went to school & saw a little baby girl being christened
(name Jeanette Mary Salt). Mr K. Richardson did it. Stayed in all night.
*P.S. Choc. Rationing starts today. We are going to visit Dad
at Totnes Friday.*

MONDAY 27   Got up 8.5. School. Prize day. Had report in morning. No homework.
Went out street for while. Am having Gran's sweets ration book for July
only. In 7.40.

JULY 1942

TUESDAY 28
Got up 7.40. School in morn. only. Breaking up for 7 weeks. In afternoon went rec to play cricket & got 9 wickets & 23 runs (2 innings 6 aside). In evening up river bank by Robin's Landing, Bag: 3 small shrimps by P. McIntosh. Home 9.15.

WEDNESDAY 29
Got up 8.20. Hols. In morning & evening played cricket up rec. total bag 7 wickets 9 runs. In afternoon went out Uncle George's for P.I. for free pass for us to go away with. Had 8d off Uncle George, Aunt Ethel & cousin Betty. Went to bed 9.30.

THURSDAY 30
Got [up] 8.50 approx. Hols. We are going away tomorrow to TOTNES to visit Dad. Did not go out street except to do errands all day. Tried to get Nat. Savings Cert. changed at P.O. but had to give 6 days notice so Nora Stephens is giving me 15/- to go away with. Bed approx 9.30.

FRIDAY 31
Got up 8.45. Hols. Got ready for journey in morning & left Newport 2.20. On way to Totnes seen 2 drones 1 loading up bombers with bombs. Arrived approx 7.30. Dad is stationed at Dartington Hall where the people are self supporting & have queer school not going if they don't like the subject & call masters Bill or Harry. Men don't have hair-cut. It is a nice place went round it with Dad. In 10.50.

signed KK

AUGUST 1942[39]

SATURDAY 1

Got up 8.30 approx. with Mam & Sylv went & walked to Totnes. I bought 1/- book on Devon & Cornwall. Had dinner at Br. Rest. On way back had a long ride 'bout 2 miles on pillion of Uncle Len Philips (?) motor cycle & after watched army sports. In evening went to Sgts. Mess. Home late hour of 12.50. Very tired. Drank 3 bottles of lemonade. We are staying with Mrs. Clements 2 doors from Co[mpan]y Office.

SUNDAY 2

[Page blotted]
Got up 9.30. Hols. Went to Paignton in morning......& came back. Spent rest of time in Sgts. Mess. Bed 11.30.

MONDAY 3

[Page blotted]
Got up 8.45. Hols. Stayed in Sgts. Mess all morning & in afternoon went to have picnic by river but just as we (Mam, Sylv & I) settled down it poured with rain so we came home. In evening Dad & I played Sgt. Rus. Jones & civilian "Dick" & lost 3 times. Home 9.45 approx.

TUESDAY 4

Got up 10.10 approx. In morning went to Totnes with Mam & Sylv & had dinner in Br. Rest & tea in Milk Bar. Went up park for while then caught last bus home & stayed in Sgts. Mess rest of time. Bed 10.20.

WEDNESDAY 5

Got up 10.15. In morning went to Totnes for dinner & I (as I came fore Mam & Sylv) had lift in R[oyal].E[ngineers]. Lorry off Sgt S. Baker R.E.. Played with S. Clements in afternoon & evening. Dad has gone to umpire a Battle & will be back tomorrow. Bed 9.0.
P.S. Had (with Mam & Sylv) some choc off Dad.

THURSDAY 6

Got up 10.15. In morning went to Totnes & had dinner in Br. Rest. Back to Dartington 3.16 approx. Mam does not feel very well[40]. Had tea in Mrs. Clements & after Mam & Sylv, Aunt May, Uncle Len, Dad & self went for row in cutter for hour. I learned to row. Had hake for supper at Sgts. Mess. Bed 9.05.

---

[39] *During the first 2 weeks of August the family stayed around the area of Totnes in Devon. Some of Ken's entries are hard to decipher as there are unfamiliar, undecipherable place names and use of initials only. Two pages are also spoiled with large ink blots. Such unclear entries will be indicated.*

[40] *Suspect Mam was in early stages of pregnancy: just over 7 months to go until 14th March 1943.*

AUGUST 1942

FRIDAY 7
Got up 11.0 approx. In morning stayed in for twas raining.
Afternoon, ditto. In evening went out to Sgts. Mess & had 3 and a half
lemonades also had cooked tea & rice pudding for tea there.
Had Meat Pie, Potatoe & Shell Peas. Bed 11.15.

SATURDAY 8
Got up 10.30. Stayed at home morn & afternoon raining. In evening after
tea went with Mam & Sylv to Sgts. Mess. Mam & Dad danced in dance
hall & Sylv & myself helped in Sgt. Bar. Got home to bed 2 AM.
Very tired.

SUNDAY 9
Got up 10.10. In morning 12.30 went to Paignton & came home 5.30.
Took own food & had tea in Milk Bar. In evening with with Mam & Sylv
to Sgts. Mess & I had 2 games of darts with Mr. Davies (L/Sgt).
1 lost easily & other lost by 4 (double 2). Home to bed 10.30.

MONDAY 10
Got up 9.5. Raining all morning & part afternoon. Went to Totnes
for dinner at B.R. & had ice at Milk Bar. Caught 3.15 bus home.
Had tea home. In evening with Mam & Dad & Sylv went for row in cutter
& Dad, a good oarsman, said I rowed O.K. At 8.15 went to Sgts. Mess
& came home 9.45.
P.S. Pinched 15 apples off tree by Sgts. Mess.

TUESDAY 11
Got up 9.50. In morning went to Totnes & had dinner at rest[aurant] in
High St costing 6/11 for dinner sweet & tea & 2 pop. But it was worth
it & all ate till full. Three-quarters of an hour later went to Milk Bar
& bought a 1/6 Knickerbocker Glory. On way back from Totnes stopped
at pontoons to watch Dad instructing men in watermanship.
Spent evening in Sgts. Mess. Home 10.30.

WEDNESDAY 12
Got up 10.0. Went to Totnes in morn. & I alone went to cinema
(3d) to see "Dead Men Tell". Caught 5.15 bus home & had tea in Sgts.
Mess. At 8.0 went to theatre to see concert which was quite good.
Home 23.00 hrs.

AUGUST 1942

THURSDAY 13
Got up 9.30. Played all morning & in afternoon with Mam & Sylv. Walked to Shinnaks Bridge & pinched plums. In evening went in Sgts. Mess & <u>may</u> have spare dart board off C.S.M. Had supper (fish) there. Pinched (alone) 7 apples. Home & bed 11.30.

FRIDAY 14
Got up 9.45. In morn with Dad went to Staverton on m[otor] bike to watch Bridging stunt. Had dinner there & got home 3.30. Had tea 4.45 & at 5 went to Sgts. Mess. Sylv & I played tennis for an hour. Left 10.50 & Dad stole 'bout 20 pears from orchard long road. Bed 11.0.

SATURDAY 15
Got up 9.35. In morning & afternoon [rained?] so stayed in & at 2.10 went to Sgts. Mess & had tea there. Had photo of Mr. G. Wilmerson (Sgt Drummer) of R.M.R.E. Band, which is being disbanded. We are going back to Newport tomorrow. Bed 12.10 very tired.

SUNDAY 16
SYLVIA'S BIRTHDAY

Got up 7.20. Sylv's birthday. I gave her 1/-. Caught 8.0 train changing at Bristol. I slept off & on in train. Got home 3.30. Out street for while. In 7.30.

MONDAY 17
Got up 9.20. Went up plot in morning & brought home 4 big lettuce, big bag full of carrots & turnips & a large cabbage. Am selling all my stamps. I had 5/- left of hols. money & now have 16/2 through stamps. Sold 'bout 200 – 300. I still have 'bout 700 – 800 left. Am selling empty album for 2/- to R. Parfitt. In 8.58 exactly.

TUESDAY 18
Got up 9.50. Sold stamps all day with I. Bowman. I sold over 5/- worth. In 8.45.

WEDNESDAY 19
Got up 9.45. Sold stamps again. This morning I sold 6/- worth have now sold 11/- worth. Aunt Elsie & twins came to tea. In 8.54.

AUGUST 1942

THURSDAY 20   Got up 9.40. In morning went up allotment & weeded. In afternoon with I. Bowman went to cinema to see "Saboteur". In evening went out street & had great fun. Bed 9.45.
P.S. Put £1 into savings.

FRIDAY 21   Got up 8.30. In morning painted grate & curb black. In afternoon as it was raining had R. Parfitt in house. In evening sold 10d of stamps to S. Packer. In 8.30.

SATURDAY 22   Got up 9.50 approx. Went salvage collecting in morning & 6 of us had 2/- twixt us, 4d each. In afternoon with D. Goulding went to cinema to see "Dive Bomber". Went out street in evening. In 8.30. Bath.

SUNDAY 23   Got up 12.30. Had breakfast in bed. Gave bike a VERY good cleaning. Went to Sunday School & in evening went out street, bought 2 pkts Ovalt[ine] tab[let]s. Man only charged me 4d for two 'stead of 8d so I weighed & weighed 6st 8lbs. In 8.15.

MONDAY 24   Got up 9.10 approx. In morning went up allotments & weeded & brought home 2 large cabs. In afternoon & evening with R. Parfitt, I. Bowman & R.P.'s little cousin Robert of 141 Corporation Rd. took tea up Tredegar Park & had great fun. Home 8.25.

TUESDAY 25   Got up 10.0. In morning helped Mam in house & at 11.0 with S. Dougan went "nutting" (collecting nuts) along Caerleon Rd & had 40 each. Home 11.40. In afternoon with Mam & Sylv went to cinema to see "The Spoilers". Home 4.30. In evening as twas raining stayed in & drew. Bed 10.15. As, as usual, we heard Farmer W. Watchet[41].

WEDNESDAY 26   Got up 10.30. In morning went out nutting but got none. In afternoon stayed in. In evening at 4.30 went to Jean Stevens party & had great fun. Had icing on cake, jelly, blancmange & batches. Home 10.5

[41.] *No idea what this relates to.*

AUGUST 1942

THURSDAY 27

Got up 10.50. In morning with W. Rackam & S. Dougan (both of Manchester St) went for ride around the streets. In afternoon stayed with Gran in house as twas too hot to go out. In evening played cricket & in 4 innings got 7 out (4 playing) & made 50 runs. In 9.5.

FRIDAY 28

Got up 9.20. In morning went up plot & brought a very large cabb & half sack full of spuds & 4 lettuce. In afternoon went out lido (Bullmore) with Sylv & J. Stevens. Took tea & had great fun. In evening stayed in.

SATURDAY 29

GRAN'S BIRTHDAY

Got up 9.50. In morning went up plot & brought half sack of spuds. In afternoon went up plot again & brought home quarter sack of spuds. In evening went to cinema to see "In Old Colorado". It rained all night & as I came home was drenched. In 8.15.

SUNDAY 30

Got up 10.50. Had breakfast in bed. In afternoon went to school. Sylv has gone back to St. Matthews. In evening stayed in.

MONDAY 31

Got up 9.10. Intended to go to Wattsville in morn with Sylv but as twas raining didn't. In afternoon went to Wattsville to see B & G Griffiths. Home 7.15. Stayed in all evening.
P.S. Mrs Lambert gave me a game of Spotto. Elementary gone back to school.

SEPTEMBER 1942

TUESDAY 1   Got up 9.30. In morning stayed in, raining. In afternoon went to cinema to see "The night of Jan 16th". Stayed in all evening as twas raining.

WEDNESDAY 2   Got up 9.35. In morning washed up & cleared table. In afternoon stayed in & at 3.30 went to Gran Clapp's. In evening went out street & had fun. In 8.45.

THURSDAY 3   Got up 9.30. In morning stayed in, afternoon ditto. In evening with R. Parfitt trailed S & A Parfitt but discovered nought. In 8.40.

FRIDAY 4   Got up 9.10. In afternoon with J. Goulding, went picking blackberries out Caerleon Field & I got a 6lb tin of flour (- flour) 2 ins from top. Got home 6.25 (J.G. earlier because of papers). Stayed in all evening. *P.S. In morn went out town.*

SATURDAY 5   Got up 9.10. At 10.5 with Sylv went to meet Brynwyn (Brinley?) Griffiths[42]. He had dinner at our house. In afternoon went to cinema to see "They Flew Alone". Home 4.40. Stayed in til 6.10 then Bryn & Sylv went in town to catch Bryn's bus to Wattsville. Went out street after, in 8.40.

SUNDAY 6   Had breakfast in bed Got up 10.45. In afternoon went to school. In evening went out street. In 9.0.

MONDAY 7   Got up 8.20. Sylv goes to school today. In afternoon went to see "N.Y. Town". In evening went out street. In 8.55.

[42.] *This person is probably a relative of Gwyneth Griffiths, perhaps younger brother, from Wattsville who married Ken's cousin Stanley Haslett.*

SEPTEMBER 1942

TUESDAY 8
Got up 8.45. In morn done errands for Mam & went up plot to bring home cabbage. In afternoon (1.35) with P. McIntosh, J. Cousins, D. Knight & another boy played soccer til 6.35 – 40. Went out street. In 9.20.

WEDNESDAY 9
Got up 8.35. In morning helped Mam. Afternoon stayed in. In evening went out street. In 8.40.

THURSDAY 10
Got up 8.15 approx. In morning helped Mam. In afternoon rode round on bike til it got a puncture. Dad is going to bring me 6 cap badges home. In evening went out street. In 8.45.

FRIDAY 11
Got up 8.40. In morn with G. Milverton & Uncle George went up uncle's plot to pull spuds. Had dinner & tea at Aunt Gert's[43]. G.M. swapped 23 badges for 150 stamps. Had great fun over there. In 8.30. Had 28 leeks off Uncle G.

SATURDAY 12
Got up 8.15. In morn went up plot to plant leeks & bring home cabbage. In afternoon cleaned my badges & buttons (58 in all). In evening went out street. In 8.50.

SUNDAY 13
Got up early to get Mam & Sylv tea & biscuits. Got up 10.15. Helped Mam for while & at 10.55 went to Aunt Phyl's. In afternoon went to school. In evening went out street. In 8.35.

MONDAY 14
Got up 8.30. In morning clipped grass for Mam. In evening went to town to buy a 5H & an H pencil value 7½d & an 8d pad. In evening went out for while. In 7.15.

---

43. *Gert Milverton, one of Dad's older sisters.*

SEPTEMBER 1942

TUESDAY 15   Got up 7.35. School. To my surprise I went into IVA instead of IVB. In evening went to cinema to see "The Lady Eve". *P.S. Mr. Fairclough is form master.*

WEDNESDAY 16   Got up 7.35. School. No homework. Went out street for while in evening. In 8.45.

THURSDAY 17   Got up 7.40. Dad came home 2.40 this morning & brought home some choc & 7 badges. School. No homework. Stayed in all night. Bed 9.15.

FRIDAY 18   Got up 7.45. School. 2 sub. for homework. In evening went out street & for a bet ran 10 times around square. After played dog & bone & Hopping Jinny. In 8.15. Bed 10.30pm.

SATURDAY 19   Got up 8.45. In morning done errands. In afternoon with Dad, Mam & Sylv went to cinema to see "Bed-Time Story". In evening stayed in. Bed 10.5 approx.

SUNDAY 20   Got up 12.5 approx but got up previously to get tea & biscuits. In afternoon went to school & I have to sing at harvest time. In evening stayed in. Bed 9.20.

MONDAY 21   Got up 7.30. School. 2 sub. for homework. Stayed in all night. Bed 9.20 approx.

TUESDAY 22   Got up 7.35. School. 1 sub. for homework. In evening went out street & had great fun. In 8.40.

SEPTEMBER 1942

WEDNESDAY 23 — Got up 7.20. School. Homework. Stayed in all night. Bed 8.50.

THURSDAY 24 — Got up 7.45. School. 1 sub for homework. Went out to play & had great fun. Bed 9.35.

FRIDAY 25 — Got up 7.30. School. 3 subs. for homework. Gwyn (Stan's wife) came from Wattsville to tea. After tea I went cinema to see "Law of the Tropics". Home 8.35. Bed late at 10.45.

SATURDAY 26 — Got up 9.15 approx. Dad has to rejoin unit today. In morning done errands for Mam. In afternoon played out back & at 4.50 approx me, I. Bowman, H. Spencer, R. Riley, C. Rogers had our names taken by Baker for going up Bakery Yard. Mam & Sylv went to station. I didn't want to go. Went out street. In 8.45.

SUNDAY 27 — Got up early to get Mam & Sylv tea. Had breakfast in bed 11.20 approx. In afternoon, school. I practised (with other children) for next week when I have to sing a song (All creatures of our God & King). Stayed in all night. Bed 8.50.

MONDAY 28 — Got up 7.40. School. 3 sub. for homework. Stayed in all night. Bed 9.40.

TUESDAY 29 — Got up 7.40. School. Homework. Stayed in all evening. Bed 8.50.

WEDNESDAY 30 — Got up 7.35. School. 3 sub. for homework. Went out street for half an hour. Bed 8.55.

signed

OCTOBER 1942

THURSDAY 1   Got up 7.25. School. 1 sub. for homework. In afternoon played form match our side lost 12-9 & their was no combination on either side & as I was extreme wing three-quarter I hardly ever got the ball from passes. Out for while. In bed 8.45.

FRIDAY 2   Got up 7.25. School. 3 sub. for homework. In evening went out street and had great fun. Played "hopping jinny". In 8.5. Bed 9.15.
P.S. Went to Lit & Deb at school.

SATURDAY 3   Got [up] 9.5. No school. At 9.45 left house to see Rugger match School XV v Bassleg XV. School won 11-6. In afternoon delivered forms for Mr. Long for old boys' serving with H[is].M[ajesty's].F[orces]. In evening stayed in. Bed 9.30 approx.
P.S. Bought marrow at Tileys Church Road for harvest.

SUNDAY 4   Got up 9.0. In morning Mam & Sylv went to Aunt Phyl's. In afternoon at 2.30 with Sylv & cousin Robbie[44] & Mam & Gran, to school where I sang a solo "All creatures of our God and King". Up Aunties for tea. Home 6.50 approx.

MONDAY 5   Got up 7.30. School. 2 sub. for homework. Stayed in all night. Bed 9.10 approx.

TUESDAY 6   Got up 7.25. School. 3 sub. for homework. At 5.20 went to Dr. Buckners to get Aunt Phyl's medicine & got back home 8.5. Had 6d off Uncle Bob for doing errand. Bed 9.20.
P.S. Dr. R. Dalziel Buckner is the name.

WEDNESDAY 7   Got up 2.50 P.M. I have very bad cold therefore stayed home from school. In all day. Bed 8.50.

[44.] *Robbie Sparkes, Aunty Phyl's elder son.*

OCTOBER 1942

THURSDAY 8
Got up 9.50 approx. Still have cold but am feeling better.
Stayed in all day. Bed 8.55.

FRIDAY 9
Got up 10.5. In morning stayed [in] & in afternoon went to cinema
to see "Moon over Burma". In evening went out street. In 7.20.

SATURDAY 10
Got up 9.35. In morn. done errands for Mam. In afternoon & evening
went out street. Went in D. Jones house. In 8.20.

SUNDAY 11
Got up early to get Mam & Sylv cup of tea. Up for good 9.20 approx.
Stayed in all morn. & in afternoon went to school. In evening went
out street. In 7.15.

MONDAY 12
Got up 7.40. School. 1 sub. for homework. Stayed in all evening.
Bed 8.57.

TUESDAY 13
Got up 7.30. School. 3 sub. for homework. In afternoon (in school hours)
I played rugby. I scored 1 try. Stayed in all evening.

WEDNESDAY 14
Got up 7.40. School. 2 sub. for homework. Stayed in all evening
as it was raining.

THURSDAY 15
Got up 7.30. School. 2 sub. for homework. I had 1/- off Aunt Gert
Milverton for my birthday. In evening went to see "Kiss the Boys
Goodbye". Home 8.35.

TOP LEFT: Cora Rosabell Haslett - Ken's 'Gran Haslett'. TOP RIGHT: Mary Blanche Clapp - Ken's 'Nana Clapp'.
BOTTOM: Ken's Father, Sergeant-Major Horace Haslett (centre, front) at Dartington Hall, Totnes, Devon.

OCTOBER 1942

FRIDAY 16

Got up 7.42. School. 3 sub. for homework. Went out street in evening & led charge v[ersus] Whitby Place & Vicinity Gang & outnumbered by 5 to 1 utterly routed them & with only 5 boys (incl self) 7 of the enemy were hurt (I hit 3 of them) & 2 were taken prisoner & their sticks given to T. Riley. A boy named Mac(Mc(?))Donald broke a stick 2 ins. in dia[meter] on boy's head. In 8.45.

SATURDAY 17

Got up 8.45. No school. It is my cousin Gladys' birthday today & I went to her party & had great fun. Home 9.40.
P.S. Had Greetings Telegram from Dad.

SUNDAY 18

Got up early to get Mam & Sylv cup of tea. Up for good 11.30. Had breakfast in bed. It is my birthday today. I am 14. Had 2/6 off Dad, 2/6 off Gran, 2/6 off Aunt Win & 5/- off Mam. School in afternoon. In all night. Bed 8.50.

MONDAY 19

Got up 7.35. School. 2 sub. for homework. In all night. Gran ill in bed with bronchitis. Bed 9.15.

TUESDAY 20

Got up 7.40. School. 3 subs. for homework. Gran is still ill, I stayed in night. Bed 9.20.

WEDNESDAY 21

Got up 7.35. School. 2 subs. for homework. In evening went to cinema to see "Great Man's Lady" & June Brooks who works there put me in the 1/6 seats for 1/- & also gave me 2 pears. Home 8.25. Gran still ill.

THURSDAY 22

Got up 7.40. School. 2 subs. for homework. Stayed in all evening. Bed 9.10.
P.S. Went to allotment after school to transplant spring cabbages. Bought half a row of them (bought 100 odd off J. Troake & Howlett for 1/-). Gran still ill.

OCTOBER 1942

FRIDAY 23   Got up 7.45. School. 3 subs. for homework. After school went to Lit.
& Deb. Sub[ject] was "Should Military training be compulsory for you?".
Vote when taken was 10 for 47 against & 1 neutral. Stayed in all evening.
Bed 9.25. Gran still ill.

SATURDAY 24   Got up early to get Mam & Sylv cup of tea. In morning went out town
with 15/6 (birthday money) to spend. Had dinner in Milk Bar.
Bought 1943 diary, 2/9 & Br. Wonderful Fighting Forces, 6/-.
Also bought choc. etc & came home with 4/5½. In evening went out
street. In 8.57. Gran still ill.

SUNDAY 25   Got up early to get Mam & Sylv cup of tea. Up for good 9.50. In afternoon
went to school. Sylv has gone back to Hereford Street Methodist (same
as me). In all evening. Bed 9.5. Gran still ill.

MONDAY 26   Got (up) 8.5. School. 1 sub. for homework. In all evening. Bed 9.10.
Gran still ill but Doctor said she is improving.

TUESDAY 27   Got up 7.35. School. 2 sub. for homework. Bed 9.15.

WEDNESDAY 28   Got up 7.35. School. 2 sub. for homework. In evening went out street. In 7.55.

THURSDAY 29   Got up 7.40. School. 1 sub. for homework. In evening went to cinema
to see "Million $ Baby". June Brooks put me in 1/6 seats for 1/-. Home 8.5.
*P.S. Squadron Leader Stenner D.F.C., D.S.O. (an old boy) paid visit to school
& spoke in hall for 5-6 minutes.*

OCTOBER 1942

FRIDAY 30

Got up 7.30. School. NO homework. Half term hols Mon[day].
After school with A. Lambert went to see his Mam's dog, black spaniel, name, Kim. Peter Butcher is leaving to join R[oyal].N[avy].
In evening (5.0) went out town to get Bacon from Fearis' & bought ink, drawing pad, ruler & 5H & HB pencil. In all night.
P.S. Am going farming tomorrow.

SATURDAY 31

Got up 7.45. I, with Potts of IVA and R. Fleet, Cartwright & Onions of IVL are going farming. Took own din[ner] & came home 6.20 approx.
Object was spud picking. We were paid 6d [per] hour & had 3/3 each.
I had ride on horse. Bed 8.55.
P.S. Gran still ill.

NOVEMBER 1942

SUNDAY 1
Got up 12.35. Had breakfast in bed. School in afternoon.
In all evening. Bed 9.10.

MONDAY 2
Got up 7.50. To go to farm (Mr. Bevan, Cefn Brethy, Cwmbran)
Mrs. B[evan] promised to meet us in car but failed to turn up.
I came back home but other 2 (F[leet] & C[artwright]) went on to farm
to find they were not wanted. To cinema to see "39 Steps".
In all evening. Sylv & Mam gone to see play which Sylv is in.
Bed 9.25. Gran still ill.

TUESDAY 3
Got up 7.35. School. 2 sub. for homework. Stayed in all evening. Bed 8.45.
P.S. Went to plot to dig & bring home cabbage for Mam. Gran still ill.

WEDNESDAY 4
Got up 7.30. School. 1 sub. for homework (has to be in Monday).
Went to cinema to see "Holiday Inn". In 8.40. Gran still ill.

THURSDAY 5
Got up 7.40. School. 1 sub for homework. Mr. Fairclough absent.
Sylv & I played 3 games of Ludo, 3 games of "Chasing Charlie" & 3 games
of Snakes & Ladders. I won by narrow margin of 5 games to 4. Broke top
off new hot-water bottle but it is still O.K. Bed 9.10. Gran still ill.

FRIDAY 6
Got up 7.35. School. 3 sub. for homework. Stayed in all evening. Bed 8.50.
P.S. Gran still ill. Sylv & I played same games as previous night.
Results same, Me 5; Sylv 4.

SATURDAY 7
Got up 8.30 approx. In morn. done errands for Mam. In afternoon
went to cinema to see "Shepherd of the hills". Home 5.35. In all evening.
Played same games as other nights. Results Sylv 5 Me 4. Total to date
Me 14 Sylv 13 (points). Bed 9.20.

NOVEMBER 1942

SUNDAY 8   Got up early to get Mam & Sylv cup of tea. Up for good 10.30.
Cleaned out my room. Sylv is ill. Gran still ill. In afternoon school.
In all evening. Bed 9.25.

MONDAY 9   Got up 7.40. School. Sylv ill. I did not go to school in afternoon because
I was ill. Dr Campbell gave Sylv medicine. Both of us have bad flu & Sylv
has neuralgia. Gran still ill. Bed 8.50.

TUESDAY 10   Got up 10.30. Slept in Mam's room cause fire was in it. ~~Dr. came to visit us~~[45]. Sylv lot better. Me worse. ~~Have to stay in bed~~. Gran still ill. Bed 8.25.

WEDNESDAY 11   ~~Got up~~ Did not get up at all today. ~~Stayed~~ 10.20 Dr. C[ampbell] came
to see us. Sylv lot better. I have to stay in bed. Gran still ill.
P.S. Mam got med[icine] off Dr for me.

THURSDAY 12   Did not get up today for I have to stay in bed. Gran & Sylv still ill. Asleep 9.5.

FRIDAY 13   Got up 3.35 P.M. Am not so ill, neither is Sylv. Dr. C[ampbell] came in
afternoon & told us we could go to school Wed but Mam said we are not
going til Mon week. Cousin Stanley Haslett is supposed to be coming home
today. Bed 8.50.

SATURDAY 14   Got up 10.30. Still upstairs in room (Mam's). Sylv & I getting down
tomorrow. Stanley came home. Gran's still ill.

SUNDAY 15   Got up 9.50. Did not go to school. In all day. Bed 8.50. Gran still ill.

---

[45] *The 'crossings-out' on these 2 days imply that Ken entered into his diary retrospectively, getting each day's events confused.*

NOVEMBER 1942

MONDAY 16   Got [up] 9.40. Am not going to school. Gran is VERY ill today
& is thought she will die [KLH: in fact Gran Haslett pulled through this
illness and eventually died in 1947 aged 79 or 80]. I had to get Dr. & get
Uncle Percy Haslett. Gran has broken muscles of back through coughing.
Stan & Gwyn (his wife) came down & were shocked. Stan is in R[oyal].
A[rtillery] signals. In all evening. Bed 9.15.
P.S. Uncle Sid Clapp is lending me his P.T. equipment.

TUESDAY 17   Got up 9.25. Am going to school tomorrow. Gran is a little better.
In morning went to Gran Clapp's, but Uncle Sid was out. In afternoon
went to cinema to see "Rookies". In all evening. Bed 8.50.

WEDNESDAY 18   Got up 7.40. School. No homework. 15 of our boys went farming.
Out street in evening. Bed 9.10. Gran still ill.

THURSDAY 19   Got up 7.45. School. 1 sub for homework. Uncle Ollie Haslett has come
to Newport to see Gran who is still ill. Went to plot in evening
& got cabbage for Mam. Out for while. In 7.40. Bed 9.10.

FRIDAY 20   Got up 7.40. School. 2 sub. for homework. Mr. Holbrook our history
master is absent. Out for while in evening. In 8.7. Bed 9.5.

SATURDAY 21   Got up 8.35. No school. In morn done errands for Mam. Got chest
expanders and wrist strengtheners off Uncle Sid + some books on P.T.
Went to cinema in afternoon to see "Navy Blues". In all evening sticking
flags & pinning them. Bought flags in morn to pin in my maps.

SUNDAY 22   Got up early to do exercises & get Mam & Sylv tea & biscuits. Played out
back in morning. In afternoon went to school & had form to get money
to relieve school dept [debt?]. In all evening. Bed 8.50.

NOVEMBER 1942

MONDAY 23   Got up 7.35. Done exercises. School. 1 sub. for homework. Had 50 lines off Evans (Prefect). In all evening. Bed 8.45.

TUESDAY 24   Got up 7.45. Done exercises. School. 1 sub. for homework. In detention for Mr. Rees. In evening went out street for while. In 6.50. Bed 9.15.

WEDNESDAY 25   Got up 7.40. Done exercises. School. 1 sub. for homework. Went to cinema to see "Remember Pearl Harbour". Home 8.35. Bed 9.15.

THURSDAY 26   Got up 8.0. Done exercises. School. 2 subs. for homework. Am in detention for Mr. D. Jones for talking. In all evening. Bed 8.40. Gran still ill.

FRIDAY 27   Got up 7.55. Done exercises. School. 3 subs. for homework. In all evening. Bed 9.10.

SATURDAY 28   Got up 8.30. Done errands for Mam in morn & went up Gran Clapps. In afternoon went to cinema to see "Somewhere in Camp". Home 5.20 approx. In all evening. Bed 8.45. Gran still ill. Done exercises.

SUNDAY 29   Got up early to get Mam & Sylv cup of tea. Up for good 9.50. Stayed in morn. School in afternoon. Took money for school 9d. In all evening. Bed 8.50. Done exercises.

MONDAY 30   Got up 7.40. Done exercises. School. 1 sub. for homework. In all evening. Bed 9.15. Gran still ill.
P.S. Went up plot to dig & transplant cabbage brought home.

DECEMBER 1942

TUESDAY 1
Got up 7.45. Done exercises. School. 3 subs. for homework. In all evening.
Gran still ill. With 6 other boys had to stay in for Mr. Fairclough
for fighting. Bed 9.10.

WEDNESDAY 2
Got up 7.45. Done exercises. Gran still ill. 1 sub. for homework. Bed 9.30.

THURSDAY 3
Got up 7.50. Done exercises. 2 sub. for homework. Gran still ill. I went
in for trials today as I may be in Tredegar B team. Came home tired.
Got kicked on head in bottom of scrum. Bed 8.40.

FRIDAY 4
Got up 7.50. School. 1 sub. for homework. Done exercises. Gran still ill.
Bed 9.10.

SATURDAY 5
Got up 8.45. No school. Done exercises. Went out town with Mam & Sylv.
I bought 3 pencils (2HBs & 5H) for I had to give Sylv 1. Also bought
4d bottle of Royal Blue ink, all cost 1/7d. Mam bought me shoes.
To Gran Clapps for dinner. Uncle Lyn Davies is home for 48 hrs again.
Went to cinema with Uncle Sid to see "Palm Beach Story". He paid
2/6 for both of us. Gran still ill. In all evening. Bed 10.30.

SUNDAY 6
Got up early to get Mam & Sylv tea & biscuits. Broke glasses yesterday.
Done exercises. Gran still ill. School. Had I.B.R.A.[46] Took 9d for Reduction
Fund. In all evening. Bed 9.10.

MONDAY 7
Got up 7.50. Done exercises. 1 sub. for homework. Mr. Fairclough
has given us (4A) all our weeks class & homework (Maths only).
In all evening. Bed 9.10.
P.S. Went in to Hudson Howards to get glasses. Price 3/6. Gran still ill.

[46.] *I.B.R.A. is probably the International Bible Reading Association. It is still active.*

DECEMBER 1942

TUESDAY 8
Got up 8.5. Done exercises. 3 sub. for homework. In all evening.
Bed 9.5. Gran still ill.

WEDNESDAY 9
Got up 7.35. Done exercises. School. No homework. Gran still ill.
Went to cinema to see "Three smart girls about town". Home 8.35.
Bed 9.15.

THURSDAY 10
Got up 7.45. School. No homework. Gran still ill. I have cold. Sylv has
cold & is home from school. In all evening. Bed 8.55. Done exercises.

FRIDAY 11
Got up 8.5. School. Sylv did not go to school for she is still ill. 1 sub. for
homework. Done exercises. Gran still ill. My cold is nearly better.
In all evening. Bed 9.10.

SATURDAY 12
Got up 8.40. No school. Done errands in morning for Mam.
Done exercises. My cold & Sylv's is better. Sylv went out to town to get
Dad birthday cards. Mam sold us 20 Players to send to Dad. Had letter
off Dad. In afternoon with D. Jones went to cinema to see "Eagle Squadron".
Home 4.10. In all evening. Bed 9.20. Gran still ill.

SUNDAY 13
Got up early to get Mam & Sylv cup of tea. Up for good 9.30.
Sunday School. 9d for reduction fund. In all evening. Bed 9.10.
Done exercises. Gran still ill.

MONDAY 14
DAD'S BIRTHDAY

Got up 7.50. School. No homework. In all evening. Have bad cold.
Done exercises. Gran still ill. Dad's birthday.

DECEMBER 1942

TUESDAY 15   Got up 11.40. Am staying home today for I was bilious (?) [Billious].
Breakfast in bed. In all day. Done exercises. Gran still ill. Wrote letter
to Dad. Bed 8.55.

WEDNESDAY 16 Got up 8.35. Did not go to school. Done exercises. Mr Wilmerson
(L/Sgt R.E.) sent me 1 of his drums. Gran still ill. In all day. Bed 8.57.
P.S. Aunt May Phillips gave us 3/- each.

THURSDAY 17   Got up 7.50. School. Done exercises. No homework. Had report
(not very good). In afternoon had entertainments in form & Wakefield
(Form Prefect) gave us a good conjuring turn. Mam is not well.
Gran still ill. Our school is breaking up tomorrow morning for 3 weeks.
In all evening. Bed 9.15.

FRIDAY 18   Got up 7.50. School in morn. Done exercises. Had aero display in morn.
Broke up for 3 weeks this morning. Gran still ill. Mam ill. In all evening.
Bed 8.50.

SATURDAY 19   Got up 9.30. No school. Done exercises. In morn done errands for Mam
who is still ill. Gran also ill. Have now 6/-. In all afternoon & evening.
Bed 9.25. Am going to buy Brits. Mod. Army (7/6) on Monday.

SUNDAY 20   Got up early to get Mam & Sylv cup of tea. Done exercises. Up for good
9.30 & lit fire. Have now 6/4d. Sunday School. In all evening. Bed 9.15.

MONDAY 21   Got up 8.45 & lit fire for Mam. Done exercises. Gran & Mam still ill.
Errands in morn & afternoon. In all evening. Bed 9.15.
P.S. Bought Br. Mod. Army.

DECEMBER 1942

TUESDAY 22   Got up 8.55. Done exercises. Gran & mam still ill. Got Mam cup of tea. Received diary (R[oyal].E[ngineers]) off Dad by post[47]. Errands in morn. Out street in afternoon & played soccer with G. Dixey, I. Bowman & J. Goulding. In all evening. Bed 9.25.

WEDNESDAY 23   Got up 8.45. Errands in morn. Had 1/- off Gran for Xmas, 2/- off Uncle Sid Clapp & 2/6 off Aunt Elsie. Gran & Mam still ill. But Mam is little better. Done exercises. Went to Ch[urch] R[oa]d Sc[hool] in afternoon & played ping-pong. In all evening & played ping-pong with Sylv for had loan of ball of[f] F. Bowman. Received Dartboard of[f] Dad. Bed 9.30.
P.S. Mam went out to buy chocs.

THURSDAY 24   Got up 8.50. Done exercises. Got Mam & Sylv cup of tea. Errands in morn & got Sylv pinafore (2/6) at Culverwells[48]. To cinema in afternoon to see "Coastal Command" with W. Simpson & I. Bowman. In all evening & played ping-pong & darts. Bed 9.35.

FRIDAY 25   Got up 8.45, to get Mam & Sylv cup of tea. Up for good 9.50. Had Atlas & lots of chocs & sweets & Mam has ordered pullover & knife from Mam's club. Chicken arrived by post from Dad. Played table-tennis & darts with Mam & Sylv, won 1½d (½d a time). Bed 9.30.
P.S. Gran still ill, but Mam is a lot better.
P.S.S. Done exercises.

SATURDAY 26   Got up 9.45. Done exercises. In all day. Bed 10.40. Gran still ill. Mam getting better.

SUNDAY 27   Got up early to get Mam & Sylv cup of tea & biscuits. Up for good, 10.15. Done exercises. Gran still ill. Mam lot better. School. Open Sunday. In all evening. Bed 9.15.

[47.] Ken had bought himself a 1943 diary on 24th October, which he used for recording 1943 events. This R.E. diary from Dad did not go to waste. Ken used it to record key events of the War in the years 1944 & 1945.

[48.] Culverwells, haberdashers shop at the junction of Church Road and Caerleon Road.

DECEMBER 1942

MONDAY 28

Got up 8.55. Done exercises. Got mam & Sylv cup of tea & biscuits & lit fire for Mam. Mam worse & Gran still ill. In morn done errands for Mam. In afternoon went to cinema to see "Front Line Kids". In all evening. Bed 9.25.

TUESDAY 29

Got up 9.10. Done exercises. Got Mam & Sylv cup of tea & biscuits & lit fire for Mam. Done errands for Mam in morn & in afternoon went up plot to dig. Home 4.40. In all evening. Gran & Mam both ill. Bed 9.35.

WEDNESDAY 30

Got up 8.55 to get Mam & Sylv cup of tea & biscuits. Done exercises. Errands in morn. Gran & Mam still ill. In morn after errands went out town & bought book for Mam. In afternoon went to cinema to see "Mayor of 44th Street". In all evening. Bed 9.10.

THURSDAY 31

Got up 10.5. Done exercises. Went to Dr. Campbell's for Mam to get medicine. Gran & Mam still ill. Dad will probably be home on leave Tuesday. In morn done errands for mam. In all afternoon & evening. Gran Clapp came to see Mam. Bed 9.35.

South Wales Argus cutting advertising films (see entry 3rd February 1943).

There are references to relatives and other bits of information that will
have been explained via footnotes in the 1942 diary. Such explanatory
notes will not be repeated for 1943 so please refer to 1942.

PERSONAL DETAILS: 1943

Name:	*K.S.HASLETT*
Address:	*42 Duckpool Road, Newport, Mon*
Identity Card No:	*XNAS III/2*
Bicycle No:	*767935*
Size in Hats:	*6 5/8*
Size in Boots:	*3 & 4*
Weight:	*7 st 3 lbs Date: 2.1.43*
Height:	*4 ft 10 ins Date: 24.10.42*

Telephone Numbers

Name	Number
Dr Campbell	*3745*
Dr. Wade Thomas	*71257*
Memorandum	
Model Supply Stores	*17, Brazennose Street, Manchester 2*

JANUARY 1943

FRIDAY 1
Got up 10.5. Done exercises. Got Mam & Sylv cup of tea & biscuits.
Lit fire for Mam. In morn went to Gran Clapp's¹ for Mam. It is raining
today. Mam & Gran Haslett still ill. In all afternoon, cleaned my room out.
In all evening. Played darts. Bed 9.25.

SATURDAY 2
Got up 8.35. Done exercises. Got Mam & Sylv tea & biscuits & lit fire.
In morn done errands. In afternoon went up Gran Clapp's for Mam.
Mam & Gran still ill. In all evening. Bed 9.15.

SUNDAY 3
Got up 9.35. Done exercises. Got Mam & Sylv tea & biscuits. Lit fire.
Gran & Mam ill, but Mam is lot better. In house all morn.
School. May go in for Bible Exam in March. In all evening. Bed 9.35.

MONDAY 4
Got up 9.10. Done exercises. Got Mam & Sylv cup of tea & lit fire.
Done errands in morn. Phoned Dr. Campbell. Gran still ill.
Mam lot better. In afternoon went to cinema to see "My Gal Sal".
Phoned Dad in evening instead of Mam, Sylv also came. Dad is coming
home approx 2.30 Wed. morn. In rest of evening. Bed 9.35.

TUESDAY 5
Got up 9.35. Done exercises. Got Mam & Sylv cup of tea. Put heater
on to warm room for Mam. Snow has fallen today. Made snowman
& snow barricade in morn & afternoon. Gran still ill. Mam prac[tically]
better. In all evening. Bed 9.25.

WEDNESDAY 6
Got up 10.10. Done exercises. Got Mam, Sylv AND Dad tea.
Dad came home 3 in morn. Errands in morn. In all afternoon
& evening. Gran still ill. Bed 10.55.

THURSDAY 7
Got up 10.35. Done exercises. Got family tea. In morn done errands
for Mam & in afternoon went to cinema with Mam, Sylv & Dad
to see "Dangerously they live". In all evening. Bed 10.40.

---

¹· *Gran Clapp's: 4 Albert Terrace, Newport*

JANUARY 1943

FRIDAY 8   Got up 7.45. School. Done exercises. No homework. In all evening. Gran still ill. Bed 10.55.

SATURDAY 9   Got up 11.35. Done exercises. In afternoon went out town. In all evening. Gran still ill. Mam better. Bed 9.50.

SUNDAY 10   Got up 10.15. Done exercises. Helped Mam in morn. School in afternoon. V. Wall, R. Price & myself as we are over 14 are not having star cards any more[2]. In all evening. Played table tennis with Dad & Sylv. Bed 9.25. *P.S. Gran still ill.*

MONDAY 11   Got up 7.45. Done exercises. School. 1 sub. for homework. Gran still ill. In all evening. Bed 9.35.
P.S. Topliss (Prefect) gave me a detention.

TUESDAY 12   Got up 7.45. Done exercises. School. 3 sub. for homework. Gran still ill. In all evening. Bed 9.45.

WEDNESDAY 13   Got up 8.5. Done exercises. School. 2 sub for homework. Gran still ill. In all evening. Bed 9.35.

THURSDAY 14   Got [up] 8.5. Done exercises. School. 1 sub. for homework. Gran still ill. In all evening. Bed 9.25.
P.S. Topliss (Prefect) put me in detention Mon[day] & I served it today.

FRIDAY 15   Got up 7.55. Done exercises. School. 2 subs for homework. Gran still ill. In all evening. Got address off H. Rudge & sent away for a 4 engined "Liberator"[3] 3/- + 4d postage. Bed 9.25.
P.S. Dad returned to unit today.

---

[2]. *A "Star card" was your Sunday School attendance record. A star was stamped on it as you turned up on a Sunday.*

[3]. *"Liberator": American 4-engined bomber*

JANUARY 1943

SATURDAY 16   Got up 8.50. Done exercises. Errands for Mam in morn. In all afternoon & evening. Gran still ill. Bed 10.0.

SUNDAY 17   Got up 10.0. Done exercises. Chopped wood for Mam in morn. School in afternoon. Mr Smith (at my request) put me up into Mr. Benzaval's class, where my pals V. Wall & R. Price are. In all evening. Gran still ill. Bed 9.25.

MONDAY 18   Got up 8.10. Done exercises. School. Gran still ill. 1 sub. for homework. In all evening. Bed 9.35.
P.S. Ordered "The Aeromodeller" in Kyrle Fletcher's.

TUESDAY 19   Got up 7.55. Done exercises. School. Gran still ill. 1 sub. for homework. Mrs. M. Jones our Fr[ench] mistress is absent. In all evening. Bed 9.35.
P.S. Mam up clinic all day so had din[ner] at Milk Bar (1/0½)

WEDNESDAY 20   Got up 7.55. Done exercises. School. Gran came downstairs today. Cousin Stan Haslett is home on leave. My "Liberator" arrived today. No homework. Done plane. Bed 9.35.

THURSDAY 21   Got up 7.45. Done exercises. School. Mr. Long our Phys[ics] Master is away. Gran down again. 1 sub. for homework. Finished aeroplane tonight. In all evening. Bed 9.25.

FRIDAY 22   Got up 7.55. Done exercises. School. Gran came down again. Stan has been recalled & has to return to his unit Sun[day]. 3 sub. for homework. In all evening. Bed 9.35.

SATURDAY 23   Got up 8.55. Done exercises. Gwyneth (Stan's wife) paid Sylv & I money for 5 weeks total 1/3 each. Had tea with Sylv & Gwyneth over Gran's. Out for while in evening. Gran down again. In 7.5. Bed 9.40.
P.S. Went up school in morn to watch our XV play Pengam: lost 9-3. See 21 Fortress bombers. [4]

---

[4] *Flying Fortress, another American 4-engined bomber*

JANUARY 1943

SUNDAY 24   Got up 9.45. Done exercises. Helped Mam in morn. Gran down again. School in afternoon. In all evening. Bed 9.25.

MONDAY 25   Got up 7.45. Done exercises. School. 2 subs. for homework. In evening went out street & played soccer with D. Goulding on my side v[ersus] W. Simpson, J. Goulding, I. Bowman & R. Parfitt. We won 21-3. I scored 19. D. Goulding 1 & I. Bowman scored against his own side. In 7.10. Bed 9.15.
P.S. Lost top off pen.

TUESDAY 26   Got up 8.10. Done exercises. School. Mr. Thomas (Dog)[5] kept form in for kicking up a row. 2 sub. for homework. Mam & Sylv went to cinema & so I washed up & cleared table. In all evening. Bed 9.35.

WEDNESDAY 27   Got up 7.50. Done exercises. School. 2 sub. for homework. ~~In all evening. Bed 9.30.~~ In evening went to cinema to see "The Lady Vanishes (Vanished?)" Home 8.15. Bed 9.30.

THURSDAY 28   Got up 8.5. Done exercises. 2 sub. for homework. School. In all evening. Bed 10.0.
P.S. I went to dance (St. Julians)

FRIDAY 29   Got up 7.50. Done exercises. School. 3 sub. for homework. In evening went out street. In 7.20. Bed 9.20.
P.S. Went to Lit. & Deb. – sub[ject] "Should prohibition be introduced?"
P.S.S. End of ITMA on Radio[6]

SATURDAY 30   Got up 9.35. Done exercises. Done errands for Mam in morn. In afternoon went to cinema to see "One foot in Heaven". In all evening. Bed 9.25.

SUNDAY 31   Got up 9.35. Done exercises. Got Mam & Sylv tea & biscuits. Mended puncture in bike & helped Mam. Did not go to school. In all afternoon and evening. Bed 9.25.

---

[5] *'Dog' Thomas was a teacher of English and, later, Economics. Good man; he got me through my 'A' Level in 1961.*

[6] *ITMA (It's That Man Again) starring Jimmy Handley was a great favourite during the early war years.*

FEBRUARY 1943

MONDAY 1
Got up 7.50. Done exercises. School. 2 sub. for homework. Dog Thomas is absent. In all evening. Bed 9.25.

TUESDAY 2
Got up 7.45. Done exercises. School. 3 sub. for homework. Dog absent. P. Doble gave me & Small of 3L 2 2d books each. In all evening. Bed 9.30.

WEDNESDAY 3
Got up 7.45. Done exercises. 1 sub. for homework. With Mam & Sylv went to cinema to see "The Forest Rangers". Home 8.45. Bed 9.20.

THURSDAY 4
Got up 7.50. Done exercises. School. 1 sub for homework. Lieut. Sharp D.S.C. R.N.V.R. gave 4th, 5th & 6th forms story of Dieppe Raid[7]. Also had 2 films, 1 about Dieppe Raid. In all evening. Bed 9.20.

FRIDAY 5
Got up 7.50. Done exercises. School. Did not go to Lit & Deb. 3 sub for homework. Went to cinema to see "Ride 'em Cowboy". Home 8.40. Bed 9.15.

SATURDAY 6
Got up 9.20. Done exercises. No school. Done errands in morn. for Mam. Chopped wood for Mam in afternoon. Had loan of "Wonders of the World" of[f] Auntie Phyl when I went there with meat in morn. Had herring off Auntie Win for tea. In all evening. Bed 9.25

SUNDAY 7
Got up 9.5. Done exercises. Got Mam & Sylv cup of tea. School. In all evening. Bed 9.20.

MONDAY 8
Got up 7.35. Done exercises. Was sick in night cos of too many sweets yesterday. Did not go to school. Got wood for Mam at King's in afternoon but stayed in all morn. In all evening. Auntie May called to see Mam. Bed 9.15.

TUESDAY 9
Got up 9.10. Done exercises. Did not go to school. In all morn & afternoon. Bed 9.15
P.S. Went over library for Sylv to get book for self. Also got ticket for self.

---

[7] *Dieppe Raid: 19 August 1942 at the French port of Dieppe a force of 5000 Canadian troops and British commandos was put ashore by landing craft to try to knock out German gun batteries and seize the port itself. The raid, supported by a massive naval bombardment and the biggest RAF operation since the Battle of Britain, was a catastrophe: 1000 Canadians killed, 2000 captured. Lessons learned from this raid aided the main invasion of Normandy in June 1944.*

FEBRUARY 1943

WEDNESDAY 10 — Got up 9.35. Done exercises. Did not go to school – still ill. In all morn except when I done errands for Mam. In afternoon went over library to join – got book for self. In evening with Mam & Sylv went to cinema to see "The Magnificent Dope". Home 8.45.

THURSDAY 11 — Got up 8.50. Done exercises. No school – ill. In all afternoon & evening. Bed 9.20.

FRIDAY 12 — Got up 8.45. Done exercises. Am lot better. Errands for Mam in morn. In afternoon went to cinema to see "Mad about Music". Out street in evening. Bed 9.10

SATURDAY 13 — Got up 9.30. Done exercises. Errands in morn. Up Gran Clapp's Uncle Lyn gave me "Recce" badge[8]. (He's in "Recce Corps"). Bough[t] 5d HB pencil 5½d protractor & 7½d pad. In afternoon made truck. Mrs. Williams[9] gave me box & wheels (box was 2d). I also bought pair of screws – 4d. In evening went out street & won 11 marbles. In 7.45. Bed 9.30.

SUNDAY 14 — Got up 10.10. Done exercises. Did not go to school in afternoon. In all evening. Bed 9.20.

MONDAY 15 — Got up 7.45. Done exercises. Thought I was going to school but was took ill – had diarrhea. In all evening. Bed 9.25.

TUESDAY 16 — Got up 7.55. Done exercises. School. 2 sub for homework. Out street for ½ hour won 8 marbles. In 7.0. Bed 9.35.

WEDNESDAY 17 — Got up 7.50. Done exercises. School. 2 sub for homework. In evening with Mam & Sylv went to cinema to see "Went the Day Well". Home 8.40. Bed 9.20.

---

[8] *Reconnaissance Corps: a newly formed Corps of small armoured vehicles designed for speedy penetration into enemy territory with force to observe and report back. Uncle Lyn Davies had applied for a transfer to this Corps from the Royal Signals and was taken on as a 2nd Lieutenant.*

[9] *Mrs Williams: next door neighbour at 41 Duckpool Road*

FEBRUARY 1943

THURSDAY 18 Got up 7.50. Done exercises. School. 2 sub for homework. Out street for while lost 2 marbles but R. Parfitt owes me 10. In 6.35. Bed 9.10.

FRIDAY 19 Got up 7.45. Done exercises. School. 2 sub for homework. ½ term on Mon[day]. In all evening. Bed 9.30.

SATURDAY 20 Got up 8.45. Done exercises. In morn with Mam & Sylv, Sylv & I had photos taken at Capitol Studios to send to Dad. In afternoon went to Harry Stevens[10] to buy a 2/6d "Authentic Model" flying "Hurricane"[11]. In all evening. Made wings of plane. Bed 9.55.

SUNDAY 21 Got up 8.35 to get Mam & Sylv tea & biscuits. Up for good 9.30. Chopped wood etc for Mam. School in afternoon. Bible lesson for those going in for Scripture Exam. In evening covered wings & doped it. Made prop & wheels. Bath. Bed 9.25.

MONDAY 22 Got up 8.35. Done exercises. No school. ½ term. In morn helped Mam got wood with my truck from King's. In afternoon went out town to buy seeds from Phillips (J). Bought Peas, Beans, Radish, Parsnip, Broc[c]oli, Savoy, Brussels Sprouts, Carrots, Beet, Swedes, Cabbage. Called up Nana Clapp's – seen twins. In evening made little bit of plane's body. Aunt May called. Bed 9.23.

TUESDAY 23 Got up 7.45. Done exercises. School. 2 sub for homework. "Fairy"[12] kept form in. "Cocky" Hyams let me & J. Whitehouse attend D. for V. Ex. On Thur with no. of others[13]. Up plot in evening. Borrowed rake of Uncle G. Milverton. In all evening. Bed 9.35

WEDNESDAY 24 Got up 7.30. Done exercises. School. No homework. Went to cinema alone to see "We'll smile again". Home 8.25. Bed 9.20.
P.S. In din[ner] hour went to get our photos.

---

[10] *Harry Stevens bike shop in Maindee Square*

[11] *Hawker Hurricane: British fighter aircraft*

[12] *"Fairy": teacher, Mr. Fairclough*

[13] *"D. for V" could be a reference to "Dig for Victory" i.e. growing your own vegetables. From entry for March 23 1942 we see that Mr Hyams is the Master in charge of allotments. No idea what the "Ex" is: Exercise? Exhibition? Exam?*

FEBRUARY 1943

THURSDAY 25   Got up 7.55. Done exercises. School. No homework. Done maths in class.
Played out back with Sylv & had great fun. In 7.25. Bed 9.25.

FRIDAY 26   Got up 7.45. Done exercises. School. 3 sub for homework.
For 1st 2 periods had Eisteddford (afternoon). In all evening. Bed 10.0.

SATURDAY 27   Got up 9.10. Done exercises. In morn. done errands for Mam & went
up Gran Clapp's. With Uncle Sid tried to do up punch-ball but didn't
have puncture outfit. In afternoon went up Uncle Jack's plot to get
7 lbs of Gen[eral] Fert[iliser] price 1/1d. Out back for while in evening.
In 7.20. Bed 9.20.

SUNDAY 28   Got up 8.45 to get Mam & Sylv tea & biscuits. Up 9.30. Done exercises.
Helped Mam in morn. School. In all evening. Bed 9.45.

MARCH 1943

MONDAY 1

Got up 7 40. Done exercises. School. No homework. Had Eisteddford in morn. ½ day in afternoon. Went up Gran Clapp's & mended puncture & dubbined[14] punch ball. Had fun. Home 6.35. In all evening. Bed 9.35.

TUESDAY 2

Got up 7.45. Done exercises. School. 2 sub for homework. In all evening. Could not do Geom[etry]. M. Lee has left. C. Drave & P. Gordon left some time ago. Bed 9.20.

WEDNESDAY 3

Got up 7.40. Done exercises. School. 2 sub for homework. Made little more of plane's body. Bed 9.20.
P.S. Up plot.

THURSDAY 4

Got up 7.35. Done exercises. School. 2 sub for homework. Mam & Sylv went to cinema to see "Road to Morocco". Bed 9.25.

FRIDAY 5

Got up 7.45. Done exercises. School. 3 sub for homework. Went to Lit & Deb. Subj[ect] was "Should Sunday entertainment be allowed?". R. (Ginger) Roberts late of VB now in our form IVA took aff[irmative]. He one [won?] 45-9 votes. Home 5.15. Out back for while in evening. In 7.30. Bed 9.35.

SATURDAY 6

Got up 8.45. Done exercises. In morn (10.15) went up school to see our 1st XV play Cathays Cardiff 1st XV. In afternoon went out town & at Arnold's bought 2 bott[les] of ink (Red & Royal Blue) & 4d mapping pen total = 1/-. In all evening. Bed 9.30.
P.S. Bought rake 2/11d.

SUNDAY 7

Got up to get Mam & Sylv tea & biscuits. Up 9.40. School. Had 2/- for prize. In all evening. Bed 9.20.
P.S. Done exercises

[14.] *"Dubbin" is a leather treatment product and used to be applied to leather footballs, football boots etc in order to provide suppleness and water-proofing. Still available today.*

MARCH 1943

MONDAY 8
Got up 7.40. Done exercises. School. 2 sub for homework. Bought spade
7/9d. In all evening. Bed 9.25.
P.S. Bought also 2ft rule 1/10d at James (where bought rake & spade).

TUESDAY 9
Got up 7.40. Done exercises. School. 2 sub for homework. New kids came
to sit today. 2nd & 3rd forms have today & tomorrow off. In all evening.
Bed 9.25.

WEDNESDAY 10
Got up 7.45. Done exercises. School. 2 sub for homework. ½ day & I took
EGG sandwiches for tea. Home 6.30. Planted 1lb (33) shallots.
Cousin Robbie (4) has measles. In all evening. Bed 9.20.

THURSDAY 11
Got up 7.40. Done exercises. School. 1 sub for homework. In all evening.
Bed 9.25.

FRIDAY 12
Got up 7.35. Done exercises. School. 3 sub for homework. Exam's start
on 25th. Had Woodie exam today – made rotten job of it, as usual.
Went up plot after school. Cocky took my ½ plot off me, leaving
me 2. Home 5.40. Bed 9.15.

SATURDAY 13
Got up early to get Mam & Sylv tea. Up 8.45. Errands for Mam in morn.
In afternoon went out town & bought Mam 2 glass tumbler & dish 1/-,
total 3/6 for birthday present. In all evening. Bed 9.35.

SUNDAY 14
Got up 9.40. Mam was taken in the night & baby was born at approx.
1.0 P.M. this afternoon. It is a BOY & is 7¼ lbs.[15] Done exercises.
Went up Gran Clapp's to tell her. Mam is OK. In all evening. Did not
go to Sunday School. I am very pleased that baby is a boy but wouldn't
have troubled if it had been a girl. Bed 9.35.

---

[15] *The birth of Keith seems to come completely out of the blue as far as Ken is concerned. When asked
many years later by Shirley (Ken's future wife of 52 years) "Didn't you know your mother was
pregnant?" Ken replied "Well nobody told me".*

Argus   March 18, 1943   5

TREATMENT OF RUSSIANS

German Atrocity Horrors

So severe were the hardships suffered by Russian peasants in occupied areas on the Smolensk front that, even when liberated by the Soviet advance, they were too dispirited to cheer even the Red Army soldiers.

They had been stripped of their belongings and lived in dug-outs in the forest hungry and cold, and the story of their plight was told by Konstantine Simonov in

LATE FOR CLASSIFICATION

To avoid the risk of loss or delay in the return of original references or other documents applicants are advised that copies only will be sufficient in the first instance

None of the vacancies for women advertised in our columns relate to a woman between 18 and 40 inclusive, unless such woman (a) has living with her a child of less than 14, or (b) is registered under the Blind Persons Acts, or (c) has a Ministry of Labour permit to allow her to obtain employment by individual effort.

A Westminster and Whittington Chiming Clock, oak case, as new, £10; Carpet Sweeper, 35/-; after 6 p.m.—27, Merlin-cres.   Q

CONFIRMATION Dress Wtd., suit girl 15.—Q 2012, Argus.   Q

CENTRAL, House for Sale, good cond., all conveniences.—Particulars, Devereux, Cambrian-rd.   Q

EXP'D Working Bailiff Req'd for small dairy farm; excellent modern house; full particulars.—Dr. McAllen, Thatch Cottage, Llanwern.

HSEMAID Req'd.—Apply Allt-yr-Yn Hospital.   Q

JACKSON'S, Ltd., have Vacancy

BIRTHS MARRIAGES DEATHS

IMPORTANT NOTICE

Advertisements of Births, Engagements, Marriages and Deaths cannot be accepted by telephone. In every case these announcements must be authenticated with the written authority and address of the sender

BIRTHDAY GREETINGS

Coulson.—To Pat, loving greetings on your birthday.—From Les, Mary and Francis.

Jones.—Loving greetings to Vily on her 13th birthday—Mam and dad. Q

Rice.—Best wishes to Charlie on his 18th birthday. Love, mam, dad, sisters and brothers.   Q

Rice.—Wishing you many happy returns of the day, Charlie, on your 18th birthday, from Aunt Polly and Uncle George.   Q

BIRTHS

Chivers.—On Mar. 16, at Kettering, to Mr and Mrs Chivers (née Vera Brown), the gift of a daughter. Q

Haslett.—On Mar. 14, at 42, Dockpool-rd., to Violet, wife of Sgt.-Major Haslett, R.M.R.E., a son.   Q

Hooper.—On Mar. 15, at 3, Watch-

TOP: Bulmore Lido open-air swimming pool visited by Ken on July 25 1943.
BOTTOM RIGHT: Cutting from the 'South Wales Argus' announcing Keith's birth, 14th March 1943.

MARCH 1943

MONDAY 15

Got up 7.40. Done exercises. School. Mam still in bed & will be in for 14 days. (Cousin) Stan is home & is at O.C.T.U.[16]. Uncle Charlie is also here from London. 2 sub for homework. In all evening. Bed 9.20.[17]

TUESDAY 16

Got up 7.20. Done exercises. School. Mam in bed. Got own breakfast & enjoyed it. In all evening. Bed 9.25.

WEDNESDAY 17

Got up 7.25. Done exercises. School. 1 sub for homework. In evening went to cinema to see "Queen Victoria" & "Old Bones of the River"[18]. Home 8.30. via Gun Platform for pinched a lift on last of 6 lorries each with a gun on back. Bed 9.20.
P.S. Made mistake with Diary entries[19]

THURSDAY 25

Got up 7.35. Done exercises. School. Dad got my breakfast today. Our form (4A) had Art exam this morning and Algebra exam in aftenoon. I think I done fairly well in Art but KNOW I done very bad in Algebra (as usual). Will be lucky if I manage to get 10%. In all evening.
P.S. Mam got out of bed for 1st time today.

FRIDAY 26

Got up 7.35. Done exercises. Dad got breakfast again. Keith is getting on fine & he & Mam came downstairs today. Had French exam this morning & Geometry exam this afternoon. Done (I think) quite well at Fr[ench] but will be lucky if I get 20%. In evening with Dad & Sylv went to cinema to see "The Pied Piper". Home 8.30. Bed 9.45.

[16.] OCTU: Officer Cadet Training Unit

[17.] No mention in the diary that this was mother's birthday (38th at the time, revised later to 40th) for which Ken had bought presents the previous Saturday

[18.] Double feature films in those days. Good value for money

[19.] What Ken had done was to inadvertently skip a week in his Diary, which resulted in him recording events for 18th to 23rd on Diary pages for the 25th to 30th. To keep in sync with his Diary I'm jumping above from Wednesday 17th to Thursday 25th, the 18th to 23rd come later

MARCH 1943

SATURDAY 27

Got up 8.40. Done exercises. Dad got my breakfast & Sylv's.
Mam & Keith downstairs again. Fluff is having kittens (Mam said).
In morn went to school pitch to see our 1st XV play Lydney Grammar
School 1st XV. Best game I have ever seen our school play.
We unfortunately lost 16-15. I think "Polly" Rowlands played best game
(full back)[20]. In afternoon took meat up Aunt Phyl's & bought 1/6d map
of Europe. In all evening. Bed 10.10.

SUNDAY 28

Got up early to get Mam, Sylv & Dad tea & biscuits. Up 9.25.
Done exercises. Helped Mam in morn. Keith had acid in him.
Did not go to school. In morning went to see Parade & met J. Whitehouse
IVB, P. Hourahaine IVB & his sister Francis (6) & G. Brown IVL.
Swotted for exam. In all evening. Bed 9.25

MONDAY 29

Got up 7.50. Done exercises. Dad got my breakfast. Had Geography
& Physics exams today. In all evening. Bed 9.40.

TUESDAY 30

Got up 7.45. Done exercises. School. Dad got breakfast for me.
Had Arith[metic] & English exams. I think (if lucky) I will get about 40%
for both. In all evening. Keith has abscess on gland.
Mam is OK. Bed 9.40.

WEDNESDAY 24

Got up 6.0 to let Dad in who came home this morning. Done exercises.
School. No homework – Swotting. Exams start tomorrow. In all evening.
Dad brought home lot of choc & other miscellaneous goods which
do not concern me but Mam. Was very pleased with Keith. Bed 10.00.

THURSDAY 18

Got up 7.25. Done exercises. No school. Had to go up clinic 'bout eyes
in morn & could not see so therefore did not go to school in afternoon.
My eyes have remained same during past year. In all evening. Bed 9.15.

FRIDAY 19

Got up 7.20. Done exercises. School. 3 sub for homework. Went up plot
after school & planted : - radish, onion (off Aunt Vi), Swede, Savoy,
Brussel Sprouts & 1 row of peas. In all evening. Bed 9.25.

---

[20]. Could this be the same John 'Polly' Rowland who later played for Newport County in the 1950s and retired to open a fish & chip shop on Corporation Road? Shirley was somehow related to this Rowland family.

MARCH 1943

SATURDAY 20 — Got up 8.40. Done exercises. No school. Errands in morn. In afternoon went to cinema to see "Footlight Serenade". Home 4.35 approx. In all evening. Mam OK Keith fine. Bed 9.40.

SUNDAY 21 — Got up early to get Mam & Sylv tea. Up 9.15. Helped Aunt Vi Attwell[21] in morn. School. In all afternoon & evening. Bed 9.35. (Done exercises).

MONDAY 22 — Got up 7.25. Done exercises. School. Got own breakfast. No homework – revision. In all evening. Bed 10.5

TUESDAY 23 — Got up 7.20. Done exercises. School. Got own breakfast. Dad is coming home tomorrow. No homework. Revision for exam. In all evening. Bed 9.10.
P.S. Went up plot to plant rest of peas & lost pen up there.
Mam is getting better & Keith is doing fine.

WEDNESDAY 31 — Got up 7.35. Done exercises. School. Got own breakfast. Had Mech., Chem[istry] & Hist[ory] exams. In evening went to cinema to see "Rookies" & "Sherlock Holmes in Washington". Home 8.25. Bed 10.45.

Signed KK

---

21. *"Aunt" Vi Attwell: Keith's Godmother. Allegedly acted as midwife through his birth*

APRIL 1943

THURSDAY 1   Got up 7.35. Done exercises. School. Got own breakfast.
Had Eng. Essay today. In all evening. K[eith]'s ~~glan~~ absis is same.
Mam O.K. In all evening. Bed 9.25.

FRIDAY 2   Got up 8.30. Done exercises. Did not go to school. Dad went back today.
Sylv & I went to see him off. I bought 1/- book:- E. of Suez, W. of Malta.
In afternoon went to see "Wake Island". Bought 2 pkt of lettuce seed.
Out street in evening. Bed 9.35.

SATURDAY 3   Got up 9.30. Done exercises. In morn went up rec with R.Parfitt,
D&J Goulding & met D&R Hassington & P.McIntosh & others
(+H. Cox). Played soccer. In afternoon went with R.Parfitt to see New-
port Youth XV v Swansea XV. We won 9-3. In all evening. Bed 9.35.
P.S. Lost knife.

SUNDAY 4   Got up 10.5. Done exercises. Had breakfast in bed. Helped Mam in morn.
Did not go to school. In all day. K[eith]'s absis is nasty.
Mam O.K. Bed 9.15.
P.S. Fluff had 2 kittens 1 born dead – Ginger. Black & white 1 alive.

MONDAY 5   Got up 7.40. Done exercises. School. No homework. In all evening.
Bed 9.25.

TUESDAY 6   Got up 7.45. Done exercises. School. 1 sub for homework. In afternoon
our form (4A) had rugger among ourselves. My side won 12-9. I scored
1 & Laux scored 3. Went to cinema to see "Powder Jane". Bed 9.20.
P.S. Had old shirt ripped off back in match.

WEDNESDAY 7   Got up 7.40. Done exercises. School. No homework. Keith was christened
at St. Matthews today. Bought over 1/- worth of books (2d's) & comics
off B.V. Edwards. In all evening. Bed 9.25.

APRIL 1943

THURSDAY 8   Got up 7.55. Done exercises. School. I was picked as outside-half
for Tredegar house XV. In afternoon our house played Beaufort
XV. B. Beech scored for us and Pook (3L) scored for Beaufort.
Final score 3-3. Had another shirt ripped of(f) back. In all evening.

FRIDAY 9   Got up 7.40. Done exercises. School. No homework. Tredegar replayed
game with Beaufort. Beaufort won 3-0. "Bunny" Austin scored.
Came home very tired. School is breaking up Wed. In all evening.
Bed 9.25.

SATURDAY 10   Got up 8.45. Done exercises. In morn. done errands for Mam. In afternoon
went up Gran Clapp's. Uncle Sid gave me a bottle of Elsocreem on condition
I always keep my hair parted. Uncle Lyn is home on leave. In all evening.
K[eith] has earache. Bed 10.5.

SUNDAY 11   Got up 9.15. Done exercises. Helped mam in morn. No school.,
did not go. In all evening. Bed 9.20.

MONDAY 12   Got up 7.55. Done exercises. School. Was late this morn. Did not
go on late-line. Beaufort v Raglan :- draw 3-3. In afternoon Abertillery
XV v Our Xv :- draw 6-6. In all evening. Bed 9.45.

TUESDAY 13   Got up 7.15. Done exercises. School. In morn Raglan v Tintern.
Raglan won 25-6(7?). In afternoon Tredegar v Beaufort. Tredegar won
45-0. Tredegar plays Raglan tomorrow. In evening went to cinema
to see "Alibi". Dr W[ade] Thomas came to see K[eith].
Home 8.35.
Bed 9.40.

WEDNESDAY 14   Got up 7.45. Done exercises. School in morn. Broke up till
May 4. Tredegar v Raglan, Tredegar won 19-3. In afternoon went
up Gran Clapp's. Had great fun with punch-ball. Had incendiary bomb
fin of[f] Gran. Now have a pair. Had tea there. Home 6.40. In all evening.
Bed 9.20.

APRIL 1943

THURSDAY 15   Got up 8.45. Done exercises. In morn got 2 loads of wood from Kings for mam (1/-) & 1 load for Mrs Ford (6d). Dug part of back in afternoon but finished when Aunt Elsie & twins came. When Aunt went D. Goulding & me dug ALL of front & pulled up rose tree. Finished 9.35. Bed 9.50.

FRIDAY 16   Got up 9.25. Done exercises. In morn helped Mam. In afternoon dug back. In evening went to cinema to see "Pride of the Yankees". It was a fine film. Home from cinema 8.35. Played rounders til 9.15. Bed 9.35.
P.S. Also went to baths in afternoon.

SATURDAY 17   Got up 8.45. Done exercises. In morn helped Mam. In house in afternoon. In evening went out street & had great fun played rounders, boys v girls. Girls :- Hazel Brooks (capt), J. Stevens, Sylvia, M. Bailey, J. Bais (Base, Baisse?), J. Adams, V. Spencer(?), J. Harry. Boys :- Me (capt), G. Dixey, L. Adams, R. Parfitt. 10 min from end D. Hill & R. Heard. I got record no. of rounders & got record no. out. In 8.50. Bed 9.35.

SUNDAY 18   Got up 8.45. Done exercises. In morn helped Mam. Did not go to school. Went up Gran Clapp's & met Aunt Elsie outside her house who was coming to see Mam with twins. I walked back home with them. In all evening. Bed 9.40.

MONDAY 19   Got up 9.10. Done exercises. In morn helped [Mam]. Ditto in afternoon. In evening went to cinema to see "Desert Victory" and "Nightmare". Home 8.10. Had good game of hot rice. In 8.30. Bed 9.25.

TUESDAY 20   Got up 8.35. Done exercises. Helped Mam in morn. In afternoon went up plot: planted marrow seed. Home 4.5. In evening went out street. Mrs. Beuzaval dragged me to Sun Ck to attend Guild. Walked out after 10 mins of it. Went out street. In 8.30. Bed 9.35.

APRIL 1943

WEDNESDAY 21   Got up 8.40. Done exercises. Helped mam in morn. In afternoon with
D, J & K Goulding & B. Lane got kicked off Girls & had great fun
on Mrs. Masters place. Home 4.35. Put line up for lady next door.
In all evening. Bed 9.30.
P.S. Went to Dr. W. Thomas' for medicine for K[eith].

THURSDAY 22   Got up 9.15. Done exercises. Helped Mam in morn. Up Masters
in afternoon & evening. Home 8.15. In rest of evening. Bed 9.25.

FRIDAY 23   Got up 9.10 . Done exercises. Helped Mam in morn. Had hot+ buns
today. Up Masters in afternoon. Had chase off bus driver next door.
Went with :- L. Adams, D&K. Goulding. In evening went out street.
Played rounders. Had great fun. I knocked 8 homers in 1 innings.
In 8.25. Bed 9.35.

SATURDAY 24   Got up 9.25. Done exercises. Helped Mam in morn. In afternoon,
with Mam, went to Bollingtons & bought sports coat & shorts grey
trousers. In evening went out street: played rounders :- R. Parfitt,
I. Bowman & I versus J. Bais, A. Parfitt, H. Brooks, L. Adams,
J. Simpson, & R. Heard. I scored 5 homers. In 8.35. Bed 9.35.

SUNDAY 25   Got up 9.35. Done exercises. Helped Mam in morn. In afternoon went
to school. In all evening. Bed 9.20.

MONDAY 26   Got up 8.50. Done exercises. Mended bike in morn. In afternoon went
to Gymkhana (Ind. Troops). In evening went out street.
In 8.30. Bed 9.20.

TUESDAY 27   Got up 9.10. Done exercises. Helped Mam in morn. In afternoon went
up Gran Clapp's. In evening played rounders, R. Parfitt, Stanley Dougan
& me versus J & D Goulding, L. Adams & Terry Flage. In 8 innings each:
score 4 – 2 homers. I scored 3, Ray 1, Derek scored both for his side.
In 8.55. Bed 9.35.

APRIL 1943

WEDNESDAY 28
Got up 9.25. Done exercises. Helped Mam in morn. Uncle Sid asked me to help him with pianos[22]. In afternoon with L. Adams went to Llanwern & also bought map of Wales & England & Wales, 6d each at K. Fletchers. Towed Les home his chain broke. Up Uncle Sid's in evening. Had 6d off him for doing nothing. Home 7.10. Bed 9.25.

THURSDAY 29
Got up 8.50. Done exercises. Helped Mam in morn. Out town in afternoon. In all evening. Bed 9.35.

FRIDAY 30
Got up 9.5. Done exercises. In morn & afternoon up Uncle Sid's. Had dinner there. Burnished hammers for him. Went round in car most of time. Home 4.35. In evening went to cinema to see "Flying Fortress". Home 9.45. Bed 10.5.
P.S. Uncle Sid gave me 2/6

---

[22] *Uncle Sid Clapp was a piano tuner*

MAY 1943

SATURDAY 1   Got up 9.35. Done exercises. Helped Mam in morn. In afternoon went out town. Spent 1d (weighed self). Changed library book. In all evening. Our wireless broke down. I went up Gran Clapp's to ask if Uncle Sid could mend it but he was not their. Bed 9.35.

SUNDAY 2   Got up 9.45. Done exercises. Helped mam in morn. In afternoon gave bike V.G. cleaning. In evening went out back & played mob with Sylv & Marie Bailey. In 8.50. Bed 9.20.
P.S. I broke my glasses.

MONDAY 3   Twins birthday[23]
Got up 9.30. Done exercises. I went to school today. In morn went up Gran Clapp's for Mam. Also posted birthday card + 5/- P[ostal].O[rder]. for twins who have whooping cough. In afternoon went to baths. In evening played rounders. In 8.50. Bed 9.25.

TUESDAY 4   Got up 7.40. Done exercises. School. 2 sub. for homework. Could not do it. Could not see. Out street. Played rounders. I. Bowman, R. Parfitt & me versus Girls:- Jean Stevens, Joan Hooper, Marie Bailey, Margery Fishwick & Sylv. 2 innings each. Boys were in (both innings) for 1½ hours. Girls in (both innings) 35 mins. In 9.10. Bed 9.40.

WEDNESDAY 5   Got up 7.40. Done exercises. School. 1 sub. for homework. Sold some of my stamps. Have now 10/1d. Johnson tried to sell me a cracked knife. Straight after school with Laux, Ashton, R.Morgan, Kennet, W. Haley, B. Rees, P. Torrington[24] & W. Alexander (4B). I got 19 runs. "Ashy" got 35 not out. Opp. Side out for 22 runs. Ours 78 all out. In 6.10. Played rounders. In 8.45. Bed 9.40.

THURSDAY 6   Got up 7.50. Done exercises. School. 1 sub. for homework. Up rec. me 31 L.B.W'd. Our side only scored 37 ALL OUT. My b(atting) av(erage) = 25 (highest). V. Peregrine knocked my shoulder. Score 37 – 9. I could not bowl. In 6.10. Had specs back. Bed 9.10.

[23.] *Twins: Peter and John Davies, sons of Lyn & Elsie (nee Clapp)*

[24.] *Ken made a note here some time later. He underlined P. Torrington and wrote at the end of the line DEAD '45.*

MAY 1943

FRIDAY 7   Got up 7.55. Done exercises. School. 3 sub. for homework.
Up rec, Wakefield, Cruikshank (Ned), L. Daniels & R. Morgan
& me (capt) v[ersus] Laux, V. Peregrine, J. Richards, J. Constable.
They were in 1st. I bowled J.C & J.R & run out Laux. All out for 68.
We went in & wanted 21 to win when it poured. I still had to go in (last).
Pulled stumps. Result:- draw. In 6.0 approx. Bed 9.20.

SATURDAY 8   Got up 8.50. Done exercises. No school. Rain all day. Done few errands.
In rest of day. Bed 9.35.

SUNDAY 9   Got up 9.10. Done exercises. Helped Mam in morn. Up Gran Clapp's
in afternoon. Seen Scout Parade. Home 4.? In rest of evening. Bed 9.40.

MONDAY 10   Got up 7.50. Done exercises. School. 2 sub. for homework. Dan Jones
kept us in but me & L. Daniels dodged him. Done chem. in school.
Went to cinema to see "ITMA" it was not so good as expected.
In 8.5. Bed 9.35.

TUESDAY 11   Got up 7.50. Done exercises. School. 2 sub. for homework. Dan put
me in detention but I had to serve the one Forbes gave me on Fri[day].
Bought H.B. pencil at Arnold's 5d & 10d of Foolscap Paper (1d per sheet).
But Mary Haines gave me 24 sheets (2/- worth). In all evening. Bed 9.40.

WEDNESDAY 12   Got up 7.55. Done exercises. School. 1 sub. for homework. Had a desk
off Gran & done homework in own room. Went to Arnold's to buy
HB Pencil, Ink, Blotting & Tracing Paper – 1/2d. In all evening. Bed 9.40.

THURSDAY 13   Got up 7.45. Done exercises. School. 2 sub. for homework. Went straight
up rec, from school after detention (D. Jones). I only got 8 runs
but bowled W & J.C. Sides:- ours, Laux, "Ned" Cruikshank, V. Peregrine
(capt) & me v[ersus] R, Morgan, Ashton, J. Constable & Wakefield.
They won 39-49. R.C. went home without inning.

MAY 1943

FRIDAY 14

Got up 7.55. Done exercises. School. Am going to try to join A. T. C's[25] (1st via B.V. Edwards). Went to plot. Brought all radish home. In all evening. Bed 9.40.

SATURDAY 15

Got up 9.40. Done exercises. Done errands in morn. Went out town. Bought note book for cadets 1/8¼d. Went up baths also changed library book. Out back with Sylv & lost ball. Bed 9.45.

SUNDAY 16

Got up & got Mam & Sylv tea & biscuits. Done exercises. Went in town to see parade & service. Done remainder of homework incl. 4 more pages of an 11 page History essay. In all evening. Bed 9.40.

MONDAY 17

Got up 7.50. Done exercises. School. 2 sub. for homework. In all evening. Bed 9.35.

TUESDAY 18

Got up 7.50. Done exercises. School. 3 sub. for homework. My lawn is coming up. In all evening. Bed 9.40.
P.S. Aunt Vi, Iris & Mo came here.

WEDNESDAY 19

Got up 7.50. Done exercises. School. No homework. ½ day for IVA & B. Went to baths in morn with IVA & went again in afternoon by self. L.R. Rowsel is going to take me to Lliswerry C.F.[26] on Friday. Went out town bought daps at Perry's & "Combined Ops" 1/- at K. Fletchers. Seen Uncle Lyn at Gran Clapp's. Went there to see if Uncle Sid had a pair of long trousers to lend me to go to C.F. In all evening. Bed 9.40.

THURSDAY 20

Gt up 8.0. Done exercises. School. 2 sub. for homework. Uncle Sid did not have any trousers. Went up from school. In all evening. My lawn is coming up fine.

[25.] *Air Training Cadets, formed in 1941 for 13 to 18 year-olds.*

[26.] *C.F. = (Army) Cadet Force for boys 12 to 18*

MAY 1943

FRIDAY 21

Got up 7.55. Done exercises. School. 3 subs. Went to Lliswerry
C.F. & am in at last! L.R.R. took me. It is at St. Andrews Inst.
Learn preliminary drill & parts of rifle. Home 9.35. Bed 10.5.
*P.S. Had 2 pairs of telegram boys trousers off Mrs Porter. May have uniform
next week. Parade on Sun[day].*

SATURDAY 22

Got up 8.50. Have cold. Done exercises. Done errands for Mam in morn.
& afternoon. In all evening. Bed 9.43.

SUNDAY 23

Got up 8.45. Done exercises. In morn went out Royal Oak to go with
C.F. Rgde. Went to Llanwern Park, had Defence v Attack. When I defended
R. Johns & I (scouts) "wiped out" party (about 8) led by Cadet C. Drave.
Went on assault course & crossed stream, barbed wire, bog, slippery pole
ditch etc. Wore D's old grey bags. Up to knees in muck. Had good time.
Home 12.35. Went to Audrey's house (198 Shafts[bury Road])
with catalogue. In rest of day. Bed 10.0.

MONDAY 24

Empire Day[27]
Got up 7.55. Done exercises. School. 2 sub. In morn. Sit Thomas Allan
came & R. Meese read his Empire Day Speech. In afternoon (½ day)
went to baths. In evening went to cinema to see "Spellbound".
It was mad[28]. Home 8.50. Bed 10.0

TUESDAY 25

Got up 7.45. Done exercises. School. 3 subs. Had to rewrite English essay
for "Dog" Thomas. Did not do Physics. At 7.0. went to Frisby's
to see 'bout uniform. Did not get it & with Ems (3B) & Griffiths am going
to be transferred from B to A Co[mpan]y (Frisby's). In rest of evening.
Bed 9.45.

WEDNESDAY 26

Got up 7.50. Done exercises. School. 1 sub. Cadets in evening
7.0. Paraded at Athletic Grounds. With Ems (3B) & Griffiths (High School)
am going to be transferred to A from B Coy. Home 8.55. Bed 9.30.

[27.] *Empire Day: instituted in 1902 on this day annually, now the 2nd Monday in March and called
Commonwealth Day. No idea who Sit Thomas Allan was.*

[28.] *Ken beginning to be a film critic. This film was about spiritualism and culminated with an exorcism.*

MAY 1943

THURSDAY 27   Got up 7.55. Done exercises. School. 1 sub. In afternoon all allotment holders finished school at 3.30. Someone pinched hoe of Mrs. Williams. Looked all round school & told boss. Home 5.40. In all evening. Bed 9.40.

FRIDAY 28   Got up 7.55. Done exercises. School. 3 subs. C.F. in evening. Griffiths has given it up "as it interferes with his school work". Sgt Richardson (VIA our school) picked on me & Ems because we came from B Coy. Made us march up & down in front of all others. Made us feel small. Made Ems give orders. H.Q. is at Frisby's. Parade Sunday. Haley (Lab Boy) is in C.F. Home 8.55. Bed 9.40.
P.S. Found HOE.

SATURDAY 29   Got up 8.50. Done exercises. Done errands in morn. In afternoon mended 2 punctures in Sylv's bike. My back inner tube is weak. In evening done some homework. Mended 2 of Sylv's punctures. Bed 9.40.
P.S. I counted 55 bombers flying very high today, probably heading E.S.E.

SUNDAY 30   Got up 8.0. Done exercises. In morn went on manoeveres again out Llanwern (met at Royal Oak). Left bike at Uncle George's (27 Hawthorn Avenue) & had lift off Beck in B Coy. Postle & 2 others tried to jump stream like me. Postle & I fell in & other tried to cross on homemade bridge – fell in. Had attack & defence. Home 2.45. In rest of day.

MONDAY 31   Got up 7.58. Done exercises. School. 2 subs. Did not do Geometry. In all evening. Bed 9.35.
P.S. When I reached school at 2.0 had to go to shelters but I did not hear siren. All clear 2.20.

JUNE 1943

TUESDAY 1

Got up 7.45. Done exercises. School. 3 subs. There was another air raid. Mrs. M. Jones said <u>SHE</u> heard the siren, but again I did not. Siren went app. 3.55. All clear 4.5. R.L. Forbes (sc[hool] capt[ain]) put me & others on "his" detention but I was determined I would not go so I did not. Iris (Attewell) came over for Sylv who had gone to Guild. In all evening. Bed 9.40.

WEDNESDAY 2

Got up 8.0. Done exercises. School. 1 sub. In evening 7.0 went to A.C.F at Frisbys. Ems did not come he went to a party. Went over Ath[letic] Gr[ound]. 2nd Lt. Owen was in a sweat when he thought 1 rifle was lost but 'twas found that only 11 were taken out. Home 9.5 app. Bed 9.45.
P.S. Went up Baths in morn with form.

THURSDAY 3

Got up 7.45. Done exercises. School. 1 sub. for homework. In all evening. Bed 9.40.
P.S. Went up plot found mattock head. Borrowed hoe & spade. Transplanted Brussel Sprouts & lettuce off[f] Ryan (IIL). Planted beans (dwarf) & beetroot. Home 7.30.

FRIDAY 4

Got up 7.50. Done exercises. School. 4 sub. Romon gave us mech. In afternoon had cricket. 1st half I made a measly 2 runs & got no-one out. Only had time for 1 over. IVL had to pull stumps after 5 min. play. A.C.F. in evening. I told adjutant that some kid has uniform in 3 days so what about me. He (Capt. Vickery) said I shall have it Wed[nesday]. There is a parade on Sun[day]. Home 9.20. Bed 10.0
On late line till 5.15 for Forbes. COMPASS.

SATURDAY 5

Got up 8.45. Done exercises. Done errands for Mam in morn, also went up baths in morn. I thought I had lost 2/6d of Mams but found it in back pocket. In afternoon went up Gran Clapps with catalogues. B[rian] S[parkes] was their [sic] as well. Home 5.35. In evening done some homework. Bed 9.40.

JUNE 1943

SUNDAY 6

Got up 7.55. Done exercises. In morn. went on manoeuvres with A.C.F.
Emms borrowed a bike & called for me. Had good time. Had verbal
messages & field signals. Home 1.57. In afternoon done more homework.
Expected Gran Clapp out but she did not come. A[untie] May came.
Emms said that his dad was in R.E's & knew my dad. In all evening.

MONDAY 7

Got up 7.50. Done exercises. School. 2 sub. In all evening. Bed 9.40.

TUESDAY 8

Got up 7.45. Done exercises. School. 3 subs. In all evening. Bed 9.50.

WEDNESDAY 9

Got up 7.45. Done exercises. School. 1 sub. Went up plot: weeded,
brought home spring cabbage. Ivor Feltham came here. He is in the D.L.I[30].
& said he has been to Tripoli from Alamein & that has been to 10 countries
in 8 yrs. He is Sgt. P.T.I[29]. Nancy came with him.
In morn. (1st period) went to baths. Boss said that in 3 weeks we shall
for 1 day have afternoon off & come to school from 6 – 9 in evening
for sports. A.C.F. in evening did not have uniform cos we are moving
to other side of road.

THURSDAY 10

Got up 7.25. Done exercises. School. 1 sub. [Cousin] Stanley [Haslett]
is home on leave & he is going to give me some chest expanders.
Dad is coming home 2.30 AM tomorrow morn – had telegram.
Reason we got up so early was cos Mam had to take Keith to see
Dr. W. Thomas. Has cricket in afternoon. I got 0. But stumped Peregrine
& Johnson (I was stumped). In all evening. Bed 9.50.
P.S. We are breaking up tomorrow morn & go back Thurs[day].

FRIDAY 11

Got up 7.55. Done exercises. School. Dad came home 3.0. this morning.
2 sub. No school in afternoon. In all evening. Bed 10.20.
P.S. I was picked to play v 4L on Wed[nesday].

---

[29] *D.L.I. – Durham Light Infantry: P.T.I. – Physical Training Instructor*

JUNE 1943

SATURDAY 12   Got up 9.35. Done exercises. In morn. [Cousin] Stan came down & Gwyn came in afternoon. Stayed with us all day. Gran came over to tea. Stan gave me a set of P.T. apparatus worth 35/- & also some P.T. books. In evening went out street. Played rounders with G.W. Dixey, J. Morgan, I. Bowman, R. Parfitt, G. Harry, S. Dougan & Sylv. I scored about 8 rounders. Busted window (middle room) with my ball in afternoon. In 9.10. Bed 11.30.

SUNDAY 13   Got up 10.10am. I started new & longer exercises today. In morn. went for walk with Dad & ?. Home 11.45. In afternoon done most of homework. In all evening. Threw stones etc at cats & got 2 with water. They were chasing Fluff. Bed 10.5.

MONDAY 14   Whit Monday
Got up 8.50. Done exercises. Took ¼ of an hour. Put best clothes [on] & at 12.5 left Newport for Wattsville. Met Stan & Gwyn at Cross Keys & walked to Wattsville. It was an awful day. Took sling & golf ball with me. Bryn & me cut golf ball in half. He is coming here Sat[urday]. Caught (Mam & Sylv & Dad & Keith) 1 min to 10 train back. Dad just came in time. Home 10.? Bed 11.20.

TUESDAY 15   Got up 9.55. Done exercises. It is raining today. In morn. went & pinched 6 of Uncle Jack's (Faulkner) golf balls & gave 3 to Gwyn. who is going to sell 'em to her boss 6d each.[30] In afternoon went to cinema to see "The Amazing Mrs Holliday". In all evening. Bed 10.35.
P.S. Dad went to Sgt Dai Davies Risca all day

WEDNESDAY 16   Got up 9.45. Done exercises. Dad got home 2.0. in morn. Done errands for Mam in morn. Mam told me she had Fluff destroyed. In afternoon 4A played 4L. We won 101 – 57 (2 innings). Played on school pitch. Mr. Butcher was ump[ire]. Me & "Crusty" Wakefield scored more than ½ between us. In 1st innings I got 11 not out & he 24 out. 2nd innings me 15 out, he 3 not out. In evening went out street. Played cricket. In 9.15. Bed 9.55. Did not go to A.C.F.

[30.] *I wonder if this bit of organised crime was a regular thing. The recipient of the stolen golf balls i.e. Gwyneth, was Cousin Stanley Haslett's first wife. One wonders if this lawless trait was cause for the eventual divorce.*

JUNE 1943

THURSDAY 17   Got up 7.50. Done exercises. School. Did not do Mecs. In evening went out street. In 8.30. Bed 8.55.

FRIDAY 18   Got up 7.40. Done exercises. School. 3 sub + mecs (to do twice). In evening went to A.C.F. & HAD UNIFORM! & everything except cape. Home 9.5. Bed 11.?

SATURDAY 19   Got up 9.15. Done exercises. In morn went out town. Bought lanyard 9d & Proberts (Khaki) renovator for gaiters 9d. Seen Uncle Arthur (Clapp). Dad is going to get me boots (Army). Brin came at 12.15 app. We went (Brin & me) to cinema to see "The Big Shot". In evening we went out on bikes. Brin went 7.30 bus. Went with him. Bed 11.35.

SUNDAY 20   Got up 8.50. Done exercises. Am starting exercises really today. Parade at Ath[letic] G[round]. Vickers water-cooled .303 M[edium] M[achine] G[un] & Sten[31]. Home 12.40. Dad went back 12.20. Left brush behind for me. Gave me & Sylv 1/- each. In all evening & afternoon. Bed 10.5

MONDAY 21   Got up 7.50. Done wrist exercises only. School. 1 sub. In evening went out street rode around with R. Parfitt. In 8.40. Bed 9.35.

TUESDAY 22   Got up 9.30. Done wrist exercises again. Overslept. Am starting exercises seriously tomorrow. Did not go school in morn. 2 sub. Stayed in for Forbes. Home 5.10. Bike – left it at Milvertons[32] on way to school tyre flat. Pumped it up & rode home. (after school). Mam presses cap (A.C.F.) & trousers. In all evening. Bed 9.30.

WEDNESDAY 23   Got up 7.50 app. Done exercises. School. 1 sub. In evening went to A.C.F. Was taught arms drill. Went to Rotary: had 1 pint of pop & slice of tart 4d. Went to baths with form this morn. Home (A.C.F.) 9.35. Bed 10.0.

[31.] *Real guns: The .303 Vickers Gun could fire over 600 rounds per minute and had a range of 4,500 yards. Being water-cooled, it could fire continuously for long periods; The Sten was a very basic weapon and was cheap and fast to manufacture. Firing 9mm ammunition it was the ideal weapon for use behind enemy lines as it used the same calibre ammunition as the German MP40.*

[32.] *Uncle George & Auntie Gert's house also in Duckpool Road, near Caerleon Road.*

JUNE 1943

THURSDAY 24

Got up 7.55. Done exercises. School. 1 sub. In dinner hour had life-saving. I cannot surface dive. Home 1.10. Had cricket in afternoon. Had opp. Side out for 19. Only Laux was out on our side. Nearly all of us had about 5 bowls. Me, Crusty & Pepper got 5 each. Crusty broke window. Ned Haley landed ball on roof. We won. Seen Tredegar v Raglan match. We won. In all evening. Bed 9.25.

FRIDAY 25

Got up 7.40. Done wrist exercises. School. 3 sub. Did not go in afternoon. Got boots 14/11d. Keith is constipated today he is not very well. Seen B.V. Edward A.C.F. in evening. Rotary: home 9.40. Bed 10.25.

SATURDAY 26

Got up 9.5. Done wrist exercises. Went to baths in morn. Home 12.0 app (I. Bowman) Out street in afternoon. Baths in evening. Home 8.? Bed 10.?

SUNDAY 27

Got up 8.25. Done wrist exercises. A.C.F. Ath[letic] Gr[ounds]. Home 1.5. Went out Bullmore Lido with Sylv, J & Y. Stevens, M. Bailey & another girl Joyce. Home 6.25. Walked to Beaufort Road. Went before Sylv & co. Bed 10.5
P.S. Did not do homework.

MONDAY 28

Got up 7.50. Done wrist exercises. School. 1 sub. Cricket in afternoon. Opp. Side 14 declared. I got 15 not out. I opened with Moggie beat them by about 10 runs & 6 wickets. Baths in evening. Can now surface dive in 6½'. Home 7.? Bed 9.40.

TUESDAY 29

Got up 7.50. Done wrist exercises. School. 2 sub. Went up rec in evening played cricket with P. McIntosh, C. Harris, "Dooda" Chilcott, J. Hassington, J. Cousins, G. Coker, R. Hayward, D. Barnes & 2 others. I got 9 runs & 1 wicket. Home 9.? Bed 10.?

WEDNESDAY 30

Got up 7.55. Done wrist exercises. School. 1 sub. Baths in morn. I was only in for 5 mins cos plaster came off sore. ½ day in afternoon. Went up Gran Clapp's. Uncle Lyn is home on emb[arcation] leave. Home 4.5. Bought 1/- worth of books (comics etc) & sold 5d. School sports in evening. Diaper, John Evans, Gilbert & Toplis broke the 4 x ¼ mile record for school. Tredegar (my house) won. Home 9.15. Bed 9.55.

100ᵗʰ (R.Mon.) Field Coy. R.E.
Darlington Hall,
Totnes.
13-12-42.

My Dear Ken,

You will perhaps be surprised to receive this from me. The reason I am writing is really to send you one of the Drums I wore on my arm.

You Ken, certainly did show great interest on the Band, & in spite of the leg pulls we had, we did try to do our best. Now our major has been posted, & the Band instruments are going back. So it is the end of the 100ᵗʰ Coy. Band, at least while the war lasts.

So Ken, I know of nobody I would care to have this Drum better than you, you will at least have

a souvenier that will remind you of the Band belonging to the Coy, which your Daddy holds the honoured position of C.S.M.

Major Everetts Son is having the other one.

Now Ken I must close, please give my kind regards to your mum & sister. Jolly good luck to you old chap.

Yours sincerely
George (Pt. Kelmerson)

Letter received by Ken along with drum badge on December 16th 1942.

JULY 1943

THURSDAY 1
Got up 7.45. Done wrist exercises. School. 1 sub. Exams next Thurs[day]. Went up rec. in evening. Played cricket. With 1 gang I got 18 not out & got hat-trick. Got 6 out. With our school boys had better game. Got 2 out in 1 over & got 7 runs b[owled]. Home 9.26. Bed 10.7.

FRIDAY 2
Got up 7.45. Done wrist exercises. School. 1 sub. A.C.F. in evening. Went in Rotary. Home 9.35. Bed 10.?
P.S. Chopped wood

SATURDAY 3
Got up 8.40. Done wrist exercises. Gwyn[neth] came for me to go up her place to see Brin. Had good time: my braces broke, had ride on Brin's bogie. In even[ing] went to Risca fair. I took 3/6 with me, spent bout 2/- & came home with 3/10. Had 2 goes on cars, 1 rifle, 1 swing, 1 round-about. Lost bout 9d-1/- on table with money. Home 8.40. Bed 9.35.

SUNDAY 4
Got up early to get tea & BISCUITS. Got up 8.40. Done wrist exercises.. A.C.F. 10am. Done Lewis (gun)[33] .300 U.S. Had sect[ion] work with L.M.S. Home 12.30. In afternoon swotted Geom[etry]. In evening out back (Keith is 4 months today (by weeks)) with Sylv played rounders. Chopped wood for Mam. In (house) 9.2. Bed 10.5.

MONDAY 5
Got up 7.55. Done wrist exercises. School. 1 sub. Went up rec. got game of cricket got about 3 out 16 runs. Home 7.15. Bed 9.50.

TUESDAY 6
Got up 7.45. Done wrist exercises. School. No homework. Went to cinema to see "Wings for the Eagle". Home 8.20. Bed 10.?. P.S. Have cold

WEDNESDAY 7
Got up 7.40. Done wrist exercises. School. Baths. Did not go to A.C.F. – swotted for exam. Bed 9.4?

---

[33] *Lewis machinegun holds the undisputable title of being first practical light machinegun, developed in 1911 in U.S.A. Had a revival in 1942 due to shortages of Bren guns.*

JULY 1943

THURSDAY 8   Got up 7.50. Done wrist exercises. School. No homework. Exams, Geom, Arith & Eng. Swotted til 7.50. Went up rec played cricket. Home 10.5. Bed 10.30.
P.S. Still have cold.

FRIDAY 9   Got up 7.50. Done wrist exercises. School. Exams, Mechs, Geog & Chem. Had assembly in evening. A.C.F. Done Lewis .300 (Yank airplane types). May be in A.C.F. cricket team. Home 9.25. Bed 9.55.

SATURDAY 10   Got up 8.50. Done wrist exercises. Done errands for Mam in morn. In afternoon went to meet Brin. I thought he had not turned up & went to cinema to se "Sundown" it was good. Got home 7.30. (Had tea at Gran Clapp's & had book on Sten of[f] Aunt Elsie). Found Brin had come early & was at cinema with Sylv. Bed 9.55.

SUNDAY 11   Got up 8.50. Done wrist exercises. Did not [go] to A.C.F. In all day – raining. Bed 10.5.

MONDAY 12   Got up 7.50. Done wrist exercises. School. No homework. Had Fr, Alg & Hist exams. Went up rec. in evening. Home 9.25. Bed 9.4.

TUESDAY 13   Got up 7.55. Done wrist exercises. School. Woodwork & Phys. Exams. Exams finish today. No homework. Went up rec. Got more than 8 out & got at least 40 runs (3 innings). Home 9.50. Bed 10.25.

WEDNESDAY 14   Got up 8.5. Done wrist exercises. School. No homework. A.C.F. in evening. Had inspection by Brig[adier]. Gen[eral] (last war). Went to Rotary. I AM in the Coy cricket team. We play B coy tomorrow. Home 9.30. Bed 10.15.

JULY 1943

THURSDAY 15   Got up 8.0. Done wrist exercises. School. No homework. Over Ath[letic] Grounds in evening, our Coy v B. We won by 2 runs. I made 18 (2 innings, 14 in 1st) & either Sgt. Coates or me had top score. Home 9.40.

FRIDAY 16   Got up 7.50. Done wrist exercises. School. No homework. Went up rec., played cricket. Got at least 3 out & made at least 14 runs. I am going to see if Wilcox have any 17/6d cricket bats tomorrow. Had cricket with school. I made 8 not out (I opened) caught 2 & stumped 1 (Stumper). Did not go to A.C.F. Home 9.35. Bed 10.5
P.S. Chucked up life-saving

SATURDAY 17   Got up 8.30. Done wrist exercises. Got Mam & Sylv tea. Out back with Sylv in morn. In afternoon (2.0) went to Wattsville to see Brin. Took 2/- with me & came back with 3/-. Spent 10d, 7d on pop (Corona) it tasted like nothing on earth could not drink it. At Cwm Brin & me bought some raspberry ice. Gave it away (went ½ each). Went to cinema at Cwm with Mr. & Mrs. Gwyn & Brin – "Mrs. Miniver". Home 9.5. Bed 9.40.
P.S. Inquired bout bat. No luck.

SUNDAY 18   Got up 9.30. Done wrist exercises. Tea for Mam & Sylv. Went over Gran's & read Stan's books. Finished one after dinner & had tea at Gran's. Went ¾ of way thro' nother 1 by 9.0. (Went over & started in morn). Home 9.0. Bed 10.5

MONDAY 19   Got up 8.10. Done wrist exercises. School. No homework. My exam average so far is somewhere around 35 (!). Up rec. in evening. Played cricket with:- A. Tovey, L. Daniel, S. Seary, W. Alexander, G. Saunders, P.D'Subin, I and S. Prince. I got 2 out L.D. & S.S. in 2 overs. Home 8.15. Bed 10.5. (Took 1 of stamp books to School).

TUESDAY 20   Got up 7.50. Done wrist exercises. School. Plots for 1st ½ of morn. Went up rec. – cricket. Got at least 3 out & made at least 30 runs (20 in 1 innings). Home 9.45. Bed 10.15.

JULY 1943

WEDNESDAY 21   Got up 7.55. Done wrist exercises. Did not go to school. Stayed home. Helped Mam in morn. Went to cinema in afternoon to see "The Black Swan". Home 4.30. Up rec in evening – cricket. Home 9.40. Bed 10.?.

THURSDAY 22   Got up 7.50. Done wrist exercises. School. No homework. Had cricket with form in afternoon. I made 8 not out. In evening went over Ath[letic] Grounds nets for practice with Coy. Home 10.5. Bed 10.35.

FRIDAY 23   Got up 7.45. Done wrist exercises. School. No homework. Bartlett said I may be in Tredegar 1st XI v Beaufort on Monday. Seen match 'tween Raglan & Tintern. Raglan won by 4 runs. E.J. Thomas broke (sprained badly?) his wrist. Brought home cabbage. Up rec. in evening. Played with G. Saunders, H. Cox, C. Watkins, M. Marels & W. Alexander (all 4B). Got 4 out made 27 runs (3 innings) & got them out in 2' & 3rd.

SATURDAY 24   Got up 8.50. Done wrist exercises. Helped Mam in morn. My report arrived. I was 22nd in exam (38.1) & 20th in homework (56). Baths in morn. Out street in afternoon. Up rec. in evening. Played cricket. Got none out made 0 runs (lousy). Home 8.55. Bed 10.5. Broke Mam's best jug.

SUNDAY 25   Got up 8.50. Done wrist exercises. Helped Mam in morn. Went out Lido with M. Watkins 1.30. Sylv & co went at 12.30. Had nice time. Had lift to Beaufort Road off C. Harris. Home 8.? Bed 10.36.

MONDAY 26   Got up 7.55. Done wrist exercises. School. Up rec in evening. Played with Grenville Williams (in Pontywain School 1st XI), P. D'Subin (in our school 1st XI), J. Laux, Chilcott(Senior) & Bunker & another. In 1 innings I made 30 declared. Chilcott made 34 out & P & J. got 7? out. Home 9.40 approx. Bed 10.20 approx.

TUESDAY 27   Got up 7.50. Done wrist exercises. School. No homework. Went up rec.

JULY 1943

WEDNESDAY 28   Got up 8.5. Done wrist exercises. School in morn. Broke up for 7 weeks.
I AM going farming 14th – 28th (August). Up baths in afternoon.
A.C.F. in evening. Had cricket practice after parade. Home 11.5. Bed 11.35.

THURSDAY 29   Got up 8.50. Done wrist exercises. No school. Helped Mam in morn.
In afternoon went to cinema to see "Commandos Strike at Dawn".
Cricket match at 7pm. Our Coy v B Coy. They won by 3 wickets
(2 innings). I made 25 runs (top) altogether. Home 10 Bed 10.30.

FRIDAY 30   Got up 9.? Done wrist exercises. Helped Mam in morn. Went to baths
in afternoon. Did not go to A.C.F. It was too hot. The tar on Caerleon
Road was melted. Went up rec. Played cricket. Home 9.30. Bed 9.50.

SATURDAY 31   Got up 8.50. Done wrist exercises. Helped Mam in morn. Mam out all
day – got own dinner. Sylv has shingles. Went to cinema in evening
to see "Invisible Agent". Home 8.40. Bed 9.40 approx.

AUGUST 1943

SUNDAY 1

Got up 9.15. Done exercises (old ones). It is lousy weather. Went up Gran Clapp's. Home 4.? In all evening. Bed 10.2.

MONDAY 2

Got up 9.50 – 10.30. Done exercises. Helped Mam & out back in morn. Went to cinema in afternoon to see "Shipyard Sally". Home 5.40. Up rec in evening. Got at least 30 runs bowled 1 caught 3 (1 of[f] own bowls). Home 9.35. Bed 9.50.

TUESDAY 3

Got up 8.40. Done exercises. Helped Mam in morn. In afternoon went for hike with D. & J. Goulding, R. Parfitt, J. Morgan, I. Flagge (?). Went by bus to Royal Oak & to Llangstone via Llanwern & back to R.O. Home 6.5. Out street in evening.

WEDNESDAY 4

Got up 9.40 approx. Done exercises. Helped Mam in morn. Went to Little Switzerland[34] with J. Morgan & I. Bowman in afternoon. Home 5.0 (it rained). Cinema in evening to see "Miss London Ltd". Home 8.52. Bed 9.35.
P.S. All of us were locked out. I went through Mr. Kidd's & let dog out. It was lost.

THURSDAY 5

Got up 9.? Done exercises. Helped Mam in morn. It is raining a lot today. Borrowed some books off Glyn Rowe. In all evening & afternoon. Bed 10.12.

FRIDAY 6

Got up 9.40. Done exercises. Helped Mam in morn. Cinema in afternoon with Sylv & Aunt Win to see "Somewhere on Leave". Aunt Win paid. Out street in evening. In 9.30. Bed 10.5.
Dog (Max) still lost. Smashed glasses.

SATURDAY 7

Got up 9.35. Done exercises. Helped Mam & played rounders in morn, afternoon & evening. In 8.55. Bed 9.45.

---

[34] *Allt-Yr-Yn, Little Switzerland*

AUGUST 1943

SUNDAY 8

Got up to get Mam & Sylv tea. No exercises. Helped Mam in morn. Lousy weather today. Lost 4 balls over Mr. Kidd's. She threw Sylv's one back & while she was talking to Mam in front I got over & found 2 of mine. Could not find my golf ball. In all evening. Bed 10.5.

MONDAY 9

Got up 8.50. Done exercises. Helped Mam in morn. Baths in afternoon. Rec in evening (up plot in morn). Home 8.55. Bed 9.45.

TUESDAY 10

Got up 9.35. Done exercises. Helped Mam in morn. Out street & playing rounders in afternoon & evening. Bed 9.40.

WEDNESDAY 11

Got up 9.20. Done exercises. Helped Mam in morn. Played rounders in afternoon & broke Mrs. Gibbs's window. Up rec in evening. Bed 9.50.

THURSDAY 12

Got up 9.10. Done exercises. Got glass for Mrs Gibbs 2/- (4d ouch) & went out town in morn. Got tooth-brush & comb & had hair-cut. Seen Percy[35] & am going to his house tomorrow to have a TENT off him. Went in town hall to see exhibits of RAF damage to enemy. Rec in afternoon. Rounders in evening. In 8.35. Bed 9.35.

FRIDAY 13

Got up 9.30. Done exercises. Had load of tent off Perce. Had bath in afternoon. Went over library & packed clothes etc for tomorrow. Went to cinema in evening to see "Transatlantic Merry-go-round".

SATURDAY 14 – FRIDAY 27

Went Farming today for a fortnight. School Camp. Llanbadoc Church Hall, Nr. Usk, Mon

SATURDAY 21

Came home for weekend. Cinema in evening to see "Look up & laugh"

SUNDAY 22

Went back 12.10.

SATURDAY 28

Came home today. Cinema in evening to see "Dr. Syn".

SUNDAY 29 – TUESDAY 31

[No entries]

signed ~~~

[35.] *Percy is probably Cousin Percy Haslett, son of Uncle George Haslett.*

SEPTEMBER 1943

WEDNESDAY 1   *[No entry]*

THURSDAY 2   Got up 10.0. Done exercises. Helped Mam in morn. In afternoon went to cinema to see "The Count of Monte Christo". Out street in evening. Bed 10.40.

FRIDAY 3   Got up 10.5. Done exercises. Helped Mam in morn. Cinema in afternoon to see "The World". A.C.F. in evening. Am taking Cert 'A'..

SATURDAY 4   Forget.

SUNDAY 5   Got up – exercises. A.C.F. in morn. In all afternoon. Played cards with Dad[36] & Sylv in evening. Won 4½d. Lost 4½d. Bed 9.55.

MONDAY 6   Got up – exercises. Went up baths in morn. Cinema in afternoon to see "My Man Godfrey". Out street in evening.

TUESDAY 7   Forget.

WEDNESDAY 8   Got – exercises. Helped Mam in morn & went up rec & played soccer with G. Saunders*, R. Fleet*, G. Seary+, Mason+, G.S's cousin & another boy & later G. Warwick+. In 2 games I scored 8 goals (5 in 1st). Cinema in afternoon to see "Hangmen also Die". It was fine. A.C.F. Am in our practice match (soccer) tomorrow.
* My age our school
+ Our school

THURSDAY 9   Got up – exercises. Tries to get some wood for Nora at King's – failed. In all afternoon. Match in evening. Home 8.30.

---

36. *Dad had come home on 10 days leave on 2nd September.*

SEPTEMBER 1943

FRIDAY 10   Got – exercises. Got wood for Nora. In all afternoon. L/Sgt Roberts
& Sgt Dai Davies had dinner here. A.C.F. in evening. Map-reading
& sequence of orders.

SATURDAY 11   Got up 8.15. Dad went back today 10.0. Bought knife without sheath
3/9d but hope to sell it for Roy Rowe offered me his pre-war 15/- sheath
knife for 7/6d. Out street in evening.
P.S. Up rec in evening played soccer (mchg. Rugger ???? 36 pts)

SUNDAY 12   Got up 8.0. Done exercises. A B & C. Coy's on march to Z Batt[ery]
on Lighthouse Road. Seen 3" U.P's & plotting room. Home 1.20.
In rest of day. Sold knife to Johnny Lewis – 3/-.
P.S. Had very heavy in night.(sic)

MONDAY 13   Got up 9.0. Done exercises. Helped Mam in morn. Out town this afternoon.
School tomorrow. I am doing paper [round] at Bainham's for 1 week
for 5/-. Out street in evening. In 7.55.
P.S. I have 6/6d towards 7/6d.

TUESDAY 14   Got up 7.45. Done exercises. I am in 5B. No homework. Out street
in evening. In 8.25.
P.S. Am doing morning papers as well for Bainham's.

WEDNESDAY 15   Got up 6.40. Done exercises. School. No homework. Done papers.
Was caught by woman inspector doing papers. Out street in evening.
P.S. BOUGHT KNIFE.
P.S. Did not go to A.C.F

THURSDAY 16   Gt up 6.50. Done exercises. Homework. In all evening.

FRIDAY 17   Got up 6.45. Done exercises & plaits[37]. Was caught by man inspector
today. 4 subs for homework. Went to A.C.F. in evening. Home 9.20
P.S. Had letter from Brin saying he was coming down tomorrow.

---

[37]. *The diary really does say 'plaits' but I have no idea what this is in this context, unless it's an early
form of 'pilates'. I don't think his hair would have been long enough for this style. Could be he just had
a minor mental gliche and meant 'papers', as he entered on subsequent days.*

SEPTEMBER 1943

SATURDAY 18   Got up 7.5. Done exercises & papers. Met Brin & we went to cinema to see "Casablanca". Had 10/- for doing papers. I had 5/- myself. Am doing just mornings next week. In all evening.

SUNDAY 19   Got up 9.0. Done exercises. A.C.F. I took squad for while. In all day.

MONDAY 20   Got up 6.35. Done exercises & papers. 2 sub for homework. In all evening.

TUESDAY 21   Got up 7.0. Done exercises & papers. Baths with form. 2 sub for homework. Went to cinema in evening to see "Meet the Stewarts".

WEDNESDAY 22   *[No entry]*

That's mainly it for 1943 entries. The odd few are as follows:

OCTOBER 1943

TUESDAY 12   Wore long trousers for first time today.

MONDAY 18   I am 15 today.

NOVEMBER 1943

TUESDAY 9   Today (with Uncle George's influence) I applied for a job at the dock's traffic dept.

WEDNESDAY 10   Today I started work (9.0am) at East Mend. (42) Box.

FRIDAY 12   Today I went to work as telephonist at the Dock's Traffic Control Office.

signed

SCHOOL HARVEST CAMP, 1943.

From August 14th to September 10th, nearly fifty boys of Upper School were in residence at Llanbadoc Church Hall, Usk. They set out every morning to help the neighbouring farmers, who again this year expressed their appreciation of our work. About £100 was earned in wages, which not only covered all camp expenses, but also nine shillings a week pocket-money for each boy. On a few evenings, the boys were invited to dancing and other entertainment at the hall of the Agricultural Institute, where a good time was had by all.

Photo & Text credit: St. Julian Magazine

TOP: A newspaper announcement regarding Ken's school visit to Llanbadoc farm, 14-27 August 1943.
BOTTOM: Llanbadoc Church Hall where 50 pupils plus their masters stayed.

1944 - 1945 DIARY ENTRIES

DIARY DATE   ENTRY

KEN ENTERED WORLD WAR EVENTS & SOME MORE LOCAL
BIKE RIDE INFORMATION IN TWO 1943 DIARIES

10 JULY 1943   **Sicily Invaded**

17 AUGUST 1943   **Sicily campaign ended**

03 SEPTEMBER 1943 Italy invaded. Italy surrenders

05 JANUARY 1944   **On approx. 5th of January 1944 I started work as messenger/stocktaker**
                   taking stock of Whiteheads Batchelors & Town Dock

04 JUNE 1944   Allies occupy Rome

06 JUNE 1944   Allies invade Europe between Cherbourg & Le Havre

13 JUNE 1944   Nazis send flying bomb over Britain

30 JUNE 1944   DAD GONE 3AM (to Normandy)

15 AUGUST 1944   Allied Troops land in Southern France between MARSEILLES & NICE

22 AUGUST 1944   Red Army enter Rumania. Paris captured by the F.F.I.
                   (the Free French Army)

31 AUGUST 1944   Red Army occupy Bucharest

1944 - 1945 DIARY ENTRIES

01 SEPTEMBER 1944   Last flying bomb over Britain (about now)

02 SEPTEMBER 1944   Allies cross Belgium border

03 SEPTEMBER 1944   British occupy Brussels

04 SEPTEMBER 1944   Russo-Finnish War ceased 8.0am today. Allies take Antwerp cutting off
enemy on French north coast (Calais etc)

05 SEPTEMBER 1944   Allies cross Luxembourg border. 7.0pm Russia declare war on Bulgaria

06 SEPTEMBER 1944   Bulgarians ask West for Armistice 12.30am

08 SEPTEMBER 1944   Russians enter Bulgaria. Bulgaria declares war on Germany

11 SEPTEMBER 1944   City of Luxembourg freed. Dutch Frontier crossed. AMERICAN TROOPS
CROSS GERMAN FRONTIER 10 MILES FROM AACHEN
AT TRIER 6.10pm

12 SEPTEMBER 1944   Allied forces in north & south of France join at Charlions cutting off
Southern & Western France

14 SEPTEMBER 1944   Red Army occupy PRAGA (Eastern suburb of Warsaw)

15 SEPTEMBER 1944   FINLAND DECLARES WAR ON GERMANY - Official

16 SEPTEMBER 1944   Enemy send over more flying bombs dropped from planes

1944 - 1945 DIARY ENTRIES

17 SEPTEMBER 1944   Blackout lifted. Allied Para & Glider Troops land in Holland (7000 - 8000 at Arnhem)

19 SEPTEMBER 1944   Brest falls after siege of about 40 days. 40,000 prisoners

22 SEPTEMBER 1944   Red Army occupy TALLINN - capital of Estonia

25 SEPTEMBER 1944   2000 of Para & Glider troops at Arnhem withdraw to Nijmegen. 1200 wounded left behind: rest - ?. They had 10 days of hell!

29 SEPTEMBER 1944   Red Army free all Estonia bar 2 islands. 30,000 enemy dead, 15,000 prisoners of war in 10 days in ESTONIA

30 SEPTEMBER 1944   Red Army enter Yugoslavia at Iron Gate & link up with Partisans

01 OCTOBER 1944   Canadians take Calais 8.0am. 7000 prisoners

02 OCTOBER 1944   British Troops land in Greece. Port of Patras occupied

02 OCTOBER 1944   8.0pm BATTLE OF WARSAW ENDS (NAZIS v PATRIOTS) AFTER 63 DAYS

05 OCTOBER 1944   ATHENS LIBERATED by Greek patriots & U.K. Troops

05 OCTOBER 1944   Red Army enter Germany's last European ally, Hungary

10 OCTOBER 1944   Czech brigade of Red Army enter own country

1944 - 1945 DIARY ENTRIES

11 OCTO BER 1944   Red Army take Cluj, capital of Transylvania

13 OCTOBER 1944   Red Army take Riga, capital of Latvia

15 OCTOBER 1944   Hungary asks for armistice

16 OCTOBER 1944   Pro-Nazi Hungarians under Szarasy take over Hungary

18 OCTOBER 1944   Nazis report Red Army in EAST PRUSSIA. No news from Russia about it

19 OCTOBER 1944   American & Australians land in Philippines

20 OCTOBER 1944   Red Army & Tito's men take BELGRADE (Yugoslavia)

20 OCTOBER 1944   U.S. Troops take AACHEN. After weeks of bitter house-to-house fighting

23 OCTOBER 1944   Russians report they are 20 miles inside EAST PRUSSIA & have taken 400 inhabited German places

25 OCTOBER 1944   Russians announce their entry into Norwegian territory: West of Petsams & clear all Transylvania

03 NOVEMBER 1944   Resistance in Scheldt pocket ends 7.30am. Therefore ALL BELGIUM FREED

04 NOVEMBER 1944   NO GERMANS IN GREECE TODAY

13 NOVEMBER 1944   TIRPITZ Sunk in Norwegian fiord by 32 Lanc & 12,000lb bombs

1944 - 1945 DIARY ENTRIES

07 JANUARY 1945   ROUTE1: ALONG CHEPSTOW ROAD TO LAWRENCE HILL:
UP LAWRENCE HILL, CROSS CHRISTCHURCH ROAD
BY MONUMENT, DOWN CAT'S ASH PATH TO CAERLEON.
ALONG CAERLEON ROAD AND HOME. APPROX DISTANCE
= 6.5 MILES (AS FROM NEWPORT BRIDGE)

07 JANUARY 1945   ROUTE2: ALONG CAERLEON ROAD TO CAERLEON. FOLLOW MAIN
ROAD TO LLANGIBBY (DISTANCE 8.5 MILES) THEN TURN LEFT
AND TAKE RIGHT FORK (General Direction WNW) FOLLOW SAME
ROAD UNTIL A POINT 0.25 MILES ABOVE NEW INN IS REACHED.
FOLLOW MAIN ROAD TO NEWPORT BRIDGE: TOTAL DISTANCE
= 17 MILES (approx)

07 JANUARY 1945   ROUTE3: FOLLOW MAIN ROAD UP STOW HILL TAKE RIGHT
FORK (RISCA) TO CROSS KEYS. TURN NORTH (still on main road)
THROUGH CWMCARN. ABERCARN, NEWBRIDGE & CRUMLIN.
TURN EAST JUST NORTH OF CRUMLIN TO PONTYPOOL.
THROUGH PONTYPOOL TAKE LEFT FORK OF MAIN ROAD TO USK.
TURN SOUTH THROUGH CAERLEON TO NEWPORT.
DISTANCE TO CROSS KEYS 10.5 MILES. CROSS KEYS TO CRUMLIN
6 MILES, CRUMLIN TO PONTYPOOL 7 MILES, PONTYPOOL
TO USK 9.5 MILES, USK TO NEWPORT 11. TOTAL 45 MILES

13 FEBRUARY 1945   ALL BUDAPEST (Hungary) IN RUSSIAN HANDS after siege 1.5 months
110,000 prisoners taken

17 FEBRUARY 1945   MACARTHUR CAPTURES BATAAN (PHILIPINES)

28 FEBRUARY 1945   MANILA FALLS (Philippines)

1944 - 1945 DIARY ENTRIES

01 MARCH 1945 U.S. TROOPS TAKE M.GLADBACH (Germany) 250,000 inhabitants

05 MARCH 1945 U.S. TANKS ENTER COLOGNE 7.0AM THIS MORNING

06 MARCH 1945 COLOGNE (3rd German City) OCCUPIED

07 MARCH 1945 U.S. TROOPS CROSS RHINE 4.30PM BETWEEN BONN & COBLENZ

08 MARCH 1945 TROOPS ENTER MANDALAY (Burmese Capital)

09 MARCH 1945 THE "LAST" OFFENSIVE STARTS IN ITALY

15 MARCH 1945 AMERICANS CAPTURE IWO JIMA (700 miles from Japan) AFTER 26 DAYS FIGHT. 5000 US MARINES DEAD, 20,000 JAPS KILLED

20 MARCH 1945 MANDALAY CAPTURED

24 MARCH 1945 21ST ARMY GROUP (THE LAST ROUND) CROSS RHINE 'tween WESEL & EMMERICH

27 MARCH 1945 LAST V2 FALLS ON ENGLAND

27 MARCH 1945 ARGENTINA DECLARE WAR ON GERMANY & JAPAN (ALL SOUTH AMERICAN REPUBLICS AT WAR WITH GERMANY & JAPAN)

28 MARCH 1945 RED ARMY TAKE GDYNIA (POLAND)

Ken's Collection of Armed Services Badges.

1944 - 1945 DIARY ENTRIES

29 MARCH 1945   RED ARMY REACH AUSTRIAN BORDER. U.S.TROOPS 80 MILES
EAST OF COLOGNE

29 MARCH 1945   U.S. TROOPS TAKE MANNHEIM (Germany)

30 MARCH 1945   RED ARMY TAKE FREE CITY OF DANZIG

01 APRIL 1945   U.S. ARMIES MEET AT LIPPSTADT THEREBY CUTTING OFF RUHR
(100,000 Germans trapped)

04 APRIL 1945   RED ARMY TAKE WIENER NEUSTADT (AUSTRIA)

08 APRIL 1945   RED ARMY ENTER VIENNA

09 APRIL 1945   KOENIGSBERG (EAST PRUSSIAN CAPITAL) TAKEN BY STORM

10 APRIL 1945   HANOVER FALLS

12 APRIL 1945   U.S. TROOPS TAKE MAGDEBURG & CROSS RIVER ELBE 60 MILES
FROM BERLIN

13 APRIL 1945   U.K. TROOPS ENTER ARNHEM (HOLLAND). VIENNA CLEARED

16 APRIL 1945   879 Enemy Planes destroyed (majority on ground)

18 APRIL 1945   2,000,000 PRISONERS (NAZI) CAPTURED SINCE D-DAY

1944 - 1945 DIARY ENTRIES

18 APRIL 1945   U.S. TROOPS ENTER CZECHOSLOVAKIA

21 APRIL 1945   BOLOGNA (ITALY) FALLS

22 APRIL 1945   RED ARMY ENTER BERLIN

25 APRIL 1945   4.40pm RED ARMY & U.S. TROOPS LINK-UP AT TORGAU

26 APRIL 1945   BERLIN CUT OFF. STETTIN FALLS. PETAIN SURRENDERS.
PATTON ENTERS AUSTRIA. ITALIAN PATRIOTS TAKE MILAN
& GENOA. ALLIED TROOPS REACH GENOA & PIACENZA.
MUSSOLINI CAPTURED. BRNO FALLS (Czechoslovakia)

27 APRIL 1945   FRENCH TAKE CONSTANCE. VERONA (ITALY) REACHED.
2ND ARMY TAKE BREMEN

28 APRIL 1945   MUSSOLINI SHOT AFTER TRIAL BY ITALIAN PATRIOTS IN MILAN

29 APRIL 1945   MUNICH & MILAN REACHED BY ALLIES. SWISS FRONTIER
REACHED BY ITALY TROOPS. GERMANS IN ITALY SURRENDER
UNCONDITIONALLY. (Land, Sea & Air Forces) All arms lain
down today

30 APRIL 1945   36 miles from RANGOON. TURIN REACHED BY U.S. TROOPS.
TWO THIRDS OF BERLIN CLEARED. TITO MEN ENTER TRIESTE

1944 - 1945 DIARY ENTRIES

30 APRIL 1945   MUNICH FALLS. RED FLAG FLIES OVER REICHSTAG (BERLIN).
MORAVA OSTRAVA FALLS (CZECHOSLOVAKIA)

30 APRIL 1945   ALLIES IN TOUCH WITH TITO'S MEN NR. TRIESTE. VENICE FALLS

30 APRIL 1945   JAPS REPORT LANDING IN BORNEO

30 APRIL 1945   DACHAU LIBERATED (after Buckenwald & BELSEN)

MAY 1945 (ACTUAL DATE UNKNOWN)   Newport - Chepstow (16) - Usk (14) - Newport (11). TOTAL = 41 miles.
5 hours easy going.

01 MAY 1945   HITLER DEAD (Report). Admiral DOENITZ said to be new Fuehrer

02 MAY 1945   ITALY: All arms lain down today 900,000 NAZIS INVOLVED.
Surrender line almost reaches Berchesgarten & includes Salzburg
& Styria (Western Austrian Provinces), excluding Trieste.
6th AIRBORNE DIV. REACH & TAKE LUBECK & WISMAR, cutting
off DENMARK, KIEL & HAMBURG. RED ARMY REACH & TAKE
ROSTOCK. ALL BERLIN CAPTURED. PARATROOPS & SEABORNE
TROOPS LAND SOUTH OF RANGOON

03 MAY 1945   HAMBURG OPEN CITY & ENTERED BY ALLIES. ENEMY NORTHERN
LINE DISINTEGRATING. 6TH AIRBORNE LINK UP WITH RUSSIANS
NEAR WISMAR (BALTIC). NEW ZEALAND TROOPS TAKE TRIESTE.
RANGOON ENTERED. PROME ENTERED. HAMBURG SURRENDERS
UNCONDITIONALLY. HALF A MILLION PRISONERS TAKEN
BY MONTY'S MEN IN 36 HOURS. KIEL CANAL CROSSED.
KIEL & FLENSBURG DECLARED OPEN CITIES

1944 - 1945 DIARY ENTRIES

04 MAY 1945   U.S. TROOPS IN AUSTRIA LINK UP WITH GEN. CLARK TROOPS
10 MILES SOUTH OF BRENNER PASS. INNSBRUCK FALLS.
SALZBURG SURRENDERS UNCONDITIONALLY. U.S TROOPS TAKE
BERCHESGARTEN. COPENHAGEN TAKEN. LINZ FALLS.
8.10pm: ALL GERMAN FORCES IN NORTH-WEST GERMANY
INCLUDING THOSE IN HOLLAND, DENMARK, HELIGOLAND
& FRISIAN ISLANDS SURRENDER TO MONTY'S 21st ARMY GROUP.
THIS TAKES EFFECT 8.0AM DBST TOMORROW. RANGOON FALLS

05 MAY 1945   1st & 19th GERMAN ARMY GROUP SURRENDER TO GEN DEVERS
7th U.S. ARMY & 1st FRENCH. SURRENDER ZONE EXTENDS FROM
JUST SOUTH OF LINZ TO SWISS FRONTIER. THIS TAKE EFFECT
TOMORROW. PATRIOTS RISE IN PRAGUE

06 MAY 1945   MOST OF PRAGUE IN PATRIOTS HANDS. PILSEN FALLS

07 MAY 1945   BRESLAU falls 40,000 prisoners. WAR REPORTED OVER.
Churchill speaks 3.0pm tomorrow.

08 MAY 1945   AT 2.41AM GEN. JODEL SIGNS UNCONDITIONAL SURRENDER
OF GERMAN LAND, SEA & AIR FORCES. Cease fire ordered yesterday.
Official end 1 minute past midnight tonight.

08 MAY 1945   PONTYPOOL - ABERGAVENNY - RAGLAN - USK - HOME.
Distance = 46 miles

12 MAY 1945   Newport to Gloucester = 46 miles; Gloucester to Cirencester = 18 miles;
Cirencester to Tetbury = 11 miles; Tetbury to Dursley = 10 miles;
Dursley to Newnham (Ferry) = 12 miles; Newnham to Newport
= 34 miles. Total = 131 miles. 2 DAYS. 16 hrs.

1944 - 1945 DIARY ENTRIES

01 MAY 1945   (Actual Date Unknown): Newport to Chepstow = 16 miles;
Chepstow to Gloucester = 30 miles; Gloucester to Ross = 18 miles;
Ross to Monmouth = 14 miles; Monmouth to Newport = 24 miles.
Total = 102 miles. 12 hours allowed look at loose leaf.

27 MAY 1945   NEXT DAY TRIP. North to Abergavenny (20) - Hereford (23)
- Monmouth (20) - Usk (13) - Newport (11). Total = 87 miles.
11 hours steady going.

21 JUNE 1945   OKINAWA 325 MILES FROM JAPAN FALLS AFTER 83 DAYS.
90,000 JAPS KILLED BY US 10th ARMY

06 AUGUST 1945   1st ATOMIC BOMB DROPPED ON JAPAN THIS MORNING. 1 = 2,000
TEN TON BOMBS. JAP TOWN (300,000 POP) is still hidden in smoke
& dust (9.0pm). £500,000,000 spent on it. Has very small explosive
content. Will in time supplement coal, oil & hydro electric power.
Commenced in U.S. in 1942.

08 AUGUST 1945   FROM TOMORROW RUSSIA IS AT WAR WITH JAPAN

08 AUGUST 1945   ALL OVER

Ken with his sister, Sylvia and brother Keith at the end of the war in the summer of 1945.

EXPLANATORY NOTES AND SUGGESTED CLASSROOM ACTIVITIES

THE RULES OF THE GAMES KEN PLAYED
By Keith Haslett, Ken's brother

SPANISH FLY - JULY 5TH 1942

This is an old leap frog game. One player is chosen to be "down". The others follow the leader in taking frog leaps over the back of the one downed. At the first leap the leader says, "Spanish fly". All the others must repeat those words upon taking their leap.

At his second leap, the leader says, "Handlings", and squeezes his fingers into the back of "Down". The others must do as he did. The leader next says, "Knucklings" and doubles his knuckles up on the back of "Down" in leaping over. The next command is "Spurrings", and the leader hits "Down" with the heel of his right foot in making the leap. The next command is "Dump the apple cart", and the leader grasps the clothes of the boy in going over and endeavors to pull him forward. The next is "Hats on deck", and the leader places his hat on the back of the boy as he passes over him. The next boy after the leader places his hat upon that of the leader and so on until all of the boys have their hats on the back.

The next command is "Hats off deck", and the last boy to place his hat upon the back is the first to leap over, endeavoring to pick his hat off without knocking any of the others off. Should any of those following the leader fail in accomplishing the trick they are supposed to do, they become "Down" and the boy who was downed becomes the leader.

www.enjoyagame.com/

EXPLANATORY NOTES AND SUGGESTED CLASSROOM ACTIVITIES

TAG & MOB - APRIL 1ST 1942

The game of "Tag" is a chasing game. Someone is "on it", they have to run around chasing the others trying to "tag" (touch) them and the person "on it" just shouts out "tag" when they've touched someone else - that person is then " on it" and the game continues as before.

"Mob" is a game of hide and seek where you "mob" a person when you find them.

DOG & BONE SEPTEMBER 18TH 1942

Use 2 sticks, one longer than the other. The short stick is pointed at one end and then laid on a stone so the pointed end stands proud. The big stick is brought down sharply on the raised end to propel the stick through the air. Whoever gets the stick furthest wins.

HOPPING JINNY SEPTEMBER 18TH 1942

Stones are laid on the ground some distance apart. The players have to hop in and out of the stones without touching them. If successful then next turn the stones are brought closer together and hopping continues. The winner is the last player to have a clear run.

SOME SUGGESTED TEACHER ACTIVITIES
Jeanette Stanley *(Ken's cousin)*

- Initial dictionary activity for unfamiliar/unknown words that may occur eg "errands"
- Whole class discussion– Show children the front cover, the foreword and the transcriber's notes including Ken's family photo and page of his actual diary. Discuss. Emphasise that Ken was a real boy who lived in Newport, South Wales. Point out the difficulties that may arise in "deciphering" Ken's diary eg " gave bike a VG cleaning"
- Use excerpts from Ken's diaries (I used 1942 Jan – June plus a few from 1943) giving one page between two children (approximately 20 diary entries); In pairs, children to scrutinise the diary and highlight (colour-code) entries made under the following four headings: Leisure time; family, friends and school; war references and ambitions/ aspirations. NB only reference made directly to ambition is Ken's desire to join the army to "do my bit for the war effort" (entry made on April 26th 1942).
- Mind Map -Using the information above, children to create a mind map about Ken using the four headings
- Diary writing – children to write a diary entry as Ken
- Role-on-the-Wall - In groups, children discuss, and record, words to describe Ken's character. Groups to feed back their words to class. Teacher record role-on-the-wall words /Children to record the role-on-the-wall in their books
- Thinking Dice - in groups, children to use the thinking dice to generate questions they would have liked to ask Ken
- Hot-Seating activity – Teacher in role as Ken, children ask their questions
- Shortburst of writing – children to create write a character sketch of Ken

- Repeat the above activities for Anne Frank's Diary
- Comparative writing - Compare Ken's war experiences to those of Anne Frank – record any similarities and differences
- Research Ken's record of war events 1943-44 – compare against Anne's diary – (powerful comparative documentation by both children); eg Ken records on 10th July 1943 "Sicily invaded" - Anne records on 11th July 1943 "the British have landed in Sicily". Also, Ken records on 4th June 1944 "Allies invade Rome" – a day later, again, Anne records ""The Fifth Army has taken Rome"
- Have a Ken day/afternoon – Ken had a very long list of leisure time activities. Let the children experience "making their own fun" as Ken did, e.g. Play cards; make jigsaws; make model airplanes (commercially bought kit or from modelling clay); play marbles; play table tennis/ping pong......the list is endless!

Printed in Great Britain
by Amazon.co.uk, Ltd.,
Marston Gate.